Patricia Rogosch, Erik Hohl

Data Protection and Facebook

Arbeitsberichte zum Informations-, Telekommunikations- und Medienrecht

Herausgegeben von

Thomas Hoeren und Bernd Holznagel

Institut für Informations-, Telekommunikations- und Medienrecht (ITM) der Westfälischen Wilhelms-Universität

Band 18

LIT

Data Protection and Facebook

An Empirical Analysis of the Role of Consent in Social Networks

by

Patricia Rogosch and Erik Hohl

LIT

Gedruckt auf alterungsbeständigem Werkdruckpapier entsprechend
ANSI Z3948 DIN ISO 9706

Bibliographic information published by the Deutsche Nationalbibliothek
The Deutsche Nationalbibliothek lists this publication in the Deutsche Nationalbibliografie; detailed bibliographic data are available in the Internet at http://dnb.d-nb.de.

ISBN 978-3-643-90250-4

A catalogue record for this book is available from the British Library

Klosbachstr. 107
CH-8032 Zürich
Tel. +41 (0) 44-251 75 05
Fax +41 (0) 44-251 75 06
e-Mail: zuerich@lit-verlag.ch
http://www.lit-verlag.ch

LIT VERLAG Dr. W. Hopf
Berlin 2012
Fresnostr. 2
D-48159 Münster
Tel. +49 (0) 2 51-620 320
Fax +49 (0) 2 51-23 19 72
e-Mail: lit@lit-verlag.de
http://www.lit-verlag.de

Distribution:
In Germany: LIT Verlag Fresnostr. 2, D-48159 Münster
Tel. +49 (0) 2 51-620 32 22, Fax +49 (0) 2 51-922 60 99, e-mail: vertrieb@lit-verlag.de

In Austria: Medienlogistik Pichler-ÖBZ, e-mail: mlo@medien-logistik.at

In Switzerland: B + M Buch- und Medienvertrieb, e-mail: order@buch-medien.ch

In the UK: Global Book Marketing, e-mail: mo@centralbooks.com

Table of Contents

1. Introduction

"We receive a number of different types of information about you, including (...)"

This sentence or alike will be found in almost every privacy policy. Once the internet user decides to become a member of a social network service (SNS) or another user generated content (UGC) website like everyone else he or she will be asked to consent to the data use policy of the respective service provider. In the unlikely case that the user actually reads the policy including the sentence mentioned above, he might wonder what the UGC provider uses his collected data for. What are the main purposes data are collected, used and disclosed for? And are these purposes clearly visible to the user? The often-cited "informed user" needs this information to give "informed consent". Therefore, this survey examines in a first part the common purposes for which UGC providers collect users' personal data (Part 1).

Consent is commonly defined as the "voluntary" agreement to the proposal of another. Before opening an account with a social network every user is supposed to ask himself if he is prepared to disclose certain personal data. In case he decides that the data he is asked for – or at least a part of it – is too personal to be used in a way described in Part 1, he might consider granting only partial consent or even not granting consent at all. But what are the consequences? In a number of cases the user will not be able to access the website at all. If he then consents to the privacy policy, can this still be regarded as "voluntary" consent? The aim of this study is to closely scrutinize the consequences of a refusal or withdrawal of consent on the user's ability to use the service (Part 2).

When analyzing the role of consent in the processing of personal data with respect to UGC one has to take into consideration that a huge part of internet users will not even read the privacy policies. The reasons for that may differ. The fact that the user consents to the policy without reading it can be due to technical difficulties in displaying the text, its accessibility or comprehensibility or simply because of its length. Hence, this survey researches into the current policies and technical features used for obtaining consent (Part 3).

The paramount objective of the project is not only to examine policies and practices in Germany, but also in other European countries such as Austria, Bulgaria, Czech Republic and others. This study is of special interest because differences between certain states can allow conclusions to be drawn about the effectiveness of legislature in the respective state and the influences on users' behavior.

This survey is based upon a European research project about consumer sentiment regarding privacy on user generated content services in the digital economy – CONSENT. This project examines the way user behavior and business practices

are changing the role of consent in the processing of personal data. CONSENT's multidisciplinary team is carrying out a status quo analysis of these practices, legal positions and consumer attitudes. It aims to identify criteria for fairness and best practices, and then create a toolkit for policy makers and corporate counsels which will enable them to address the problems identified in the analysis.
The views and opinions expressed in this publication only reflect the authors' point of view and not necessarily those of CONSENT and the European Commission.

2. Methods used for research

2.1 Analysed UGC services

Within this survey 140 UGC websites (national internet appearances) of 107 UGC service providers were analysed. Internationally operating service providers often use different specifications for their websites under different country domains. While the base frame of the websites may be generally identical, there can be slight or distinct varieties in presentation and content, especially regarding the presentation of the terms of services and the privacy policies. For example, a few project partners reported that the privacy policy is displayed partly or fully in foreign language. Since this is only one example for likely differences in the national appearances of internationally operating UGC service providers, the total number of 140 services to be examined contains several national appearances of the same internationally operating UGC service provider (for example *Wikipedia* and *Facebook*). Thus, "140 services in total" means for the following survey a total of 140 web appearances, which contains multiple national appearances of some of the internationally operating UGC service providers.

Additionally to those national appearances of internationally operating UGC service providers, 17 "international" UGC service providers are surveyed which offer one website but target users in multiple countries (like *Facebook.com, youtube.com or flickr.com*).

Considering this, the 140 UGC services which are to be examined are composed of the following:

Austria: studiVZ.de, schuelerVZ.de, xing.com, elitepartner.at, Szene1, secondlife

Bulgaria: sibir.bg, bg-mamma.com, impulse.bg, contacto.bg, elmaz.com, vbox7.com, bgrabotodatel.com, edno23.com, bg.wikipedia.org, hanovete.com

Czech Republic: lidé.cz, Spolužáci.cz, Doktorka, Jobs.cz, Líbímseti.cz, Rajče.net, Česko-slovenská filmová databáze, Teidu, Osobnosti.cz, GamePark

Denmark: Facebook.com, jubii.dk, support.emu.dk, arto.dk, dating.dk, youtube.com, alatest.dk, da.wikipedia.org

France: windows live spaces, Copains d'avant, friendsclear, Viadeo, Meetic.fr, skyrock, LeGuide, eRepublik

Germany: Facebook.com, meinVZ.de, StudiVZ.de wer-kennt-wen.de, schuelerVZ, Topmedic.de, elitepartner.de, Youtube.com, spickmich.de, imedo, Twitter.com, blogdsld.com, exika, World of Warcraft

Italy: me2.it, crohniani.it, link2me.it, theclub.it, diggita.it, lastfm.it, meemi.com, nonciclopedia.it, terrediextramondo.com

Malta: skolaĦbieb.com

Netherlands: hyves.nl, schoolbank.nl, legal360, relatieplanet.nl, Picasa.com, kieskeurig.nl, zoover.nl, twitter.com, wikipedia.org, World of Warcraft

Poland: nasza-klasa.pl, grono.net, epuls.pl, goldenline.pl, sympatia.onet.pl, fotka.pl

Romania: neogen.ro, Desprecopii.com, Clopotel.ro, Tetatet.ro, Sentimente.ro, Trilulilu.ro, Cirip.ro, Wikipedia, Triburile.ro

Slovakia: diskusneforum.sk, azet.sk, spoluziaci.sk, esvety.sk, sexifotky.sk, pcforum.sk, birdz.sk, dailychat.sk, facebook.com, wikipedia.org, hi5.com, bebo.com

Spain: Facebook.com, Flickr, Tuenti, 4networking, eDarling, Youtube, Spotify, Twitter, Wikipedia, Second Life

United Kingdom: friendsreunited.com, Mumsnet, Date Positive, LinkedIn, eHarmony.co.uk, Flickr, AutoTrader, Twitter, Wikipedia, World of Warcraft

International: Facebook.com, myspace.com, classmates, gays.com, Xing.com, Linkedin.com, parship.com, Flickr.com, Youtube.com, last.fm, Tripadvisor, yelp.com, Twitter, Wikipedia, myheritage, Secondlife.com, World of Warcraft

2.2 Examining the UGC services

When answering the questions, partners were asked to proceed as follows: if a certain criterion applied to the UGC service being examined, the respective column was to be filled out with a "1", in order to simplify the later processing of the results. Where a criterion did not apply, the column was to remain blank. It is worth noting that in some cases more than one answer was correct or applicable. Additionally, it was possible that none of the mentioned answers were adequate. In this case partners were able to use the "Other" column and explain how the UGC provider deals with the issue in question. Wherever one of the provided answers appeared to fit to a certain extent, partners were advised to select that specific answer. Moreover, each question had a column named "Comment". This "Comment" column was created for any additional comments or explanations regarding one of the answers listed. Polar questions with one "Answer" column only, were to be answered by filling in a "1" for "yes" and leaving the column blank for a "no".

3. Areas of examination

In order to effectively conduct the study, the following aspects of gaining consent were examined. As previously stated, the questionnaire used for the survey is dividedinto three different parts.

The first part, which consists of five questions, focuses on the common purposes for which service providers collect, use or disclose personal data. How the providers communicate these purposes to the user and where in the privacy policy the purposes are mentioned are important aspects to be analysed in this part.

The second part of the questionnaire, which contains a total of nine questions, entails numerous questions, related to the withdrawal, respectively the refusal of consent and the consequences that are possibly linked to it.

The third and final part, which consists of ten questions, deals with the identification of policies and technical features that are being used by the providers for obtaining consent. This part covers, amongst other things, technical features, appearance, accessibility and comprehensibility of the privacy policy.

The significant amount of data collected via the survey gives an instructive view on the current policies and practices of the UGC providers for obtaining consent.

3.1 Part 1: Common purposes for which UGC service providers collect, use and disclose users' personal data

Users' consent is only informed when they know about the purposes for which the UGC service providers collect, use and disclose their personal data. If users do not know what their data are used for, they can hardly reasonably decide if they are willing to consent or not. Part one of this survey deals with the aspect of purposes for which the provider collects personal data. It was analysed what the main purposes for which data are collected, used and disclosed are. Furthermore, it was examined how the purposes are being communicated to the user and where the information about the purposes is found in the privacy policy or terms of service. In addition to that, the different kinds of user data were examined and it was determined whether different types of data are used for different purposes. The final objective of part one was to find out if the UGC service providers inform the user that third parties are involved as well. It is important to notice that research could only be based on the documents available on the services' websites. The fact that a service does not point out a specific purpose leaves it possible that the service provider still uses the data for that very purpose, but does not inform the user of this fact.

3.1.1 Collection, usage and disclosure of data – What are the main purposes?

3.1.1.1 Explanation

For consent to be informed, it is necessary that the user is given information regarding the purposes for which data are collected. Information on this could be found in the privacy policy, respectively the terms of service or related documents. It is of general interest what the main purposes for the collection of data are.

Categories of possible answers:

a) To profile the user with a view to make profit
b) To fulfill legal obligations
c) To contact users
d) For statistical reasons
e) In order to verify users' age
f) To enable features on the website to function
g) For transactions/payments
h) To enable search engines not affiliated with the provider to access information
i) Other
j) Comment

Further information on the purposes:

a) This includes ads by the provider itself and ads placed by third parties.
b) Laws may require providers to save IP numbers and to disclose them to law enforcement agencies under specific circumstances.
c) Reasons for this are manifold; the provider might want to send promotional material or may only want to let users know about technical problems with the website etc.
d) This may include an analysis of the overall traffic to direct server capacities, to find out which parts of the service are being used frequently and which parts are not etc.
e) This may come up, as some services may require users to be at least of a certain age.
f) Those features could include users' ability to search for friends using the service specific search engine or to enable them to suggest friends etc.

g) If the service charges for the service, it might be necessary to collect payment information. That information may be handed over to banks in order to carry out the transaction.

h) This can be the case if the user allows the service to let external search engines access his or her profile.

3.1.1.2 Results of examination

Doc. 1

Member State	To profile the user with a view to make profit	To fulfill legal obligations	To contact users	For statistical reasons	In order to verify users' age	To enable features on the website to function	For transactions/ payments	To enable search engines not affiliated with the provider to access information	Other	No purposes mentioned (e.g. there is no privacy policy nor ToS, there is privacy policy or terms of service but purposes are not mentioned)
Austria	0	5	1	1	5	1	0	1	1	0
Bulgaria	5	7	8	5	3	8	1	1	3	1
Czech Republic	1	2	8	1	0	3	0	1	0	2
Denmark	5	5	4	3	4	7	0	3	0	1
France	4	7	8	6	5	8	6	1	0	0
Germany	7	9	8	11	3	9	3	4	4	2
Italy	2	2	1	4	0	4	3	1	2	3
Malta	0	0	0	0	0	0	0	0	0	1
Netherlands	3	4	5	2	0	8	4	0	0	1
Poland	6	6	6	6	6	5	4	2	0	0
Romania	6	7	8	8	1	7	3	0	2	0
Slovakia	0	12	8	5	5	7	1	1	3	0
Spain	10	9	10	9	6	9	2	0	0	0
United Kingdom	2	0	3	8	5	6	3	3	0	2
International	14	14	16	11	3	17	4	1	2	0
	65	89	94	80	46	99	34	19	17	13

Conducting the research, it became quite obvious that UGC service providers use personal data for many different purposes - according to their own declarations. However, there are not many significant differences in the usage of purposes. Most purposes can be found in many different UGC services. Data were used most commonly in order to enable features on the website of the service to function (71% or 99 out of 140 services under scrutiny). This purpose was widely mentioned in all member states except for Austria and the Czech Republic. It was also used by all of the 17 international services. The importance of it is rather unsurprising, as almost all data collected for UGC services can be used in order to enable features on the services' websites. For example, contact information on a social network service can be used for users to search each other on the website, uploading a video on a content share enables other users to view it etc. The purpose of contacting users (67% or 94 out of 140 services), the fulfilment of legal obligations (64% or 89 out of 140 services), and statistical reasons (57% or 80 out of 140 services) were almost just as common purposes used by the UGC service providers. The purpose of contacting users was rarely used in Austria and Italy, but was used more often in virtually all other member states.The significance of this purpose is due to the fact that almost all UGC services may need to contact their users at some point. However, it has to be taken into consideration that virtually only contact information is used in order to contact users. Thus, the purpose does not have any significance as to other purposes. The situation regarding the fulfillment of legal obligations can somewhat be compared to that one. This purpose is of great importance in almost all member states, but the statistics dealing with this purpose must also be regarded with caution. The reason for this is the fact, that some data may be collected because of legal obligations. In contrast to that, providers may not be required to collect certain data, but if they do so, they may be forced to turn it over to law enforcement authorities. Moreover, there are some exceptions as to the distribution of the purposes among the various member states. This purpose is not mentioned in either of the websites under scrutiny in the United Kingdom and hardly in the Czech Republic and Italy. The reason for this is not clear, but it seems to make sense that there is a link to the legal situation in those respective member states. The same is true as to statistical purposes. Those purposes were mentioned quite often in all member states. However, in Austria, the Czech Republic, Denmark and the Netherlands the share was a little lower than in other member states. Other widely mentioned purposes were the profiling of users for commercial reasons (46% or 65 out of 140 services) and the verification of users' age (33% - 46 out of 140 services). Interestingly, the usage of the former purpose varies starkly between the different member states. While it was mentioned by all Spanish services and 14 out of 17 international services, it was not mentioned at all in Slovakia and Austria and hardly mentioned in the Czech Republic, Italy, the Netherlands and the United Kingdom. It is also of importance to notice that it is not unlikely that a significant number of services do not state the purpose of profiling users with the intention to make profits. This is due to the fact that this purpose is the most important purpose related to generating income for UGC services. However, some income is also generated with data collected for statistical reasons, as this may include the demographics of the users of the various services. These data can be used to make the service more attractive for advertising that does not have to be personalized. The usage of the latter purpose varies similarly from member state to member state. While it was used by 70% of the Spanish services, it was not used at all by services in the Czech Republic, the Netherlands and Italy and only by one service in Romania. Further purposes identified in the preliminary research and confirmed by the various partners were the usage of the personal data for transactions and payments (24% - 34 out of 140 services) and the purpose of allowing search engines not affiliated with the service access the users' information (14% - 19 out of 140 services). The usage for personal data for transactions and payment is only that low because not that many UGC services under scrutiny offer services with costs.

However, further purposes were identified by the various member states. Some of those purposes are quite similar to those that were listed prior to the research. Many services stated, for example, that they use the data in order to improve the service. This is quite similar to statistical purposes, because those statistics are likely to be used to improve the service. The same is true with the purpose of solving technical problems, but this purpose could also be categorized under "enabling features on the websites to function". Due to the similarity of those purposes with the purposes already listed above, those are of lesser importance. Another purpose mentioned by various providers is the purpose of defending the network against attacks by hackers. This purpose can hardly be categorized under any of the listed categories and is of some significance itself. Other purposes mentioned were administrative purposes and "providing a social environment related advertisement to friends". The latter can probably also be categorized under "profiling the user in order to make profit".

3.1.2 Informed user or obscured purposes?

3.1.2.1 Explanation

It is not only important to analyse what the main purposes are but also how the UGC service provider is communicating these purposes to the users. Is the user informed directly and explicitly that the provider is, for example, collecting data for profiling the user with a view to make profit out of it? Or is the provider perhaps describing the purpose ambiguously or using fancy words? In that case it is not very likely to be clear to the user what the UGC service provider is actually doing with his or her personal data. Thus, it cannot be assumed that the user is clearly informed. He or she is not fully aware of what might happen with his or her data. Last but not least, it is also possible that the UGC service provider is not mentioning at all in the privacy policy or in the terms of service what he is doing with the data collected. If this is the case, it is possible that he is either not using the data for a certain purpose or he is concealing to the user about the real purpose for which he is collecting the data.

Categories for possible answers:

a) To profile the user with a view to make profit

b) To fulfill legal obligations

c) To contact users

d) For statistical reasons

e) In order to verify users' age

f) To enable features on the website to function.

g) For transactions/payments.
h) To enable search engines not affiliated with the provider to access information.
i) Other
j) Comment

Note: This question had to be answered differently to the other ones. For each purpose the partners had to write in the column whether the purpose is explained directly, obscured or not mentioned at all. If the purpose is told by the provider in an obscured way, the partners were to write down the sentence in the column as well. This question aimed mainly at the language used by UGC service providers in order to inform users of the purposes data are collected for. It was of high interest whether the language used permits average users to understand the purposes.

Categories to fill in:

a) Explained directly = 1
b) Obscured + sentence that describes the purpose
c) Not mentioned at all: please leave the column blank

Example:
Doc. 2

Name of UGC service	To profile the user with a view to make profit	To fulfill legal obligations	To contact users	For statistical reasons	In order to verify users' age	To enable features on the website to function	For transactions/ payments	To enable search engines not affiliated with the provider to access informatio	Other	Comment
wer-kennt-wen.de	obscured; I agree that studivz uses my data (the ones I communicated during registration, the	directly	directly	obscured	directly					

3.1.2.2 Results of examination

Doc. 3

Member state	To profile the user with a view to make profit	To fulfill legal obligations	To contact users	For statistical reasons	In order to verify users' age	To enable features on the website to function	For transactions/ payments	To enable search engines not affiliated with the provider to access information	Other	No purposes mentioned (e.g. there is no privacy policy nor ToS, there is privacy policy or terms of service but purposes are not mentioned)
Austria	0	5	1	1	3+2 obscured	1	0	1	1	0
Bulgaria	3+ 2 obscured	7	3+5 obscured	4+1 obscured	2+1 obscured	4+ 4 obsured	1	1	3	1
Czech Republic	1	2	8	1	0	1+2 obscured	0	1 obscured	0	2
Denmark	5	5	4	3	4	7	0	3	0	1
France	3+1 obscured	7	8	5+1 obscured	5	8	6	1	0	0
Germany	4 +3 obscured	9	7+ 1 obscured	9+2 obscured	3	6+3 obscured	3	3+1 obscured	4	2
Italy	2	2	1	4	0	4	3	1	2	3
Malta	0	0	0	0	0	0	0	0	0	1
Netherlands	3	4	5	2	0	8	4	0	0	1
Poland	6	6	6	6	6 obscured	5	1+3 obscured	2	0	0
Romania	2+4 obscured	7	8	3+5 obscured	1	5+2 obscured	3	0	2	0
Slovakia	0	12	8	5	5	7	1	1	3	0
Spain	10	9	10	9	6	9	2	0	0	0
United Kingdom	2	0	3	8	5	6	3	3	0	2
International	11+3 obscured	14	16	11	3	17	4	1	2	0
	52+13 obscured	89	88+6 obscured	71+9 obscured	37+9 obscured	88+11 obscured	31+3 obscured	17+2 obscured	17	13

Doc. 4

Member State	Directly explained	Obscured	Total
Austria	13	2	15
Bulgaria	28	13	41
Czech Republic	13	3	16
Denmark	31	0	31
France	43	2	45
Germany	48	10	58
Italy	19	0	19
Malta	0	0	0
Netherlands	26	0	26
Poland	32	9	41
Romania	31	11	42
Slovakia	42	0	42
Spain	55	0	55
United Kingdom	30	0	30
International	79	3	82
	490	53	543

The examination of question two of part one led to clear results that were not necessarily expected. It was found that the vast majority of UGC services do not try to obscure the purposes for which they collect personal data at all. The services tend to directly state why they collect the data, providing they state the purposes in the privacy policy or the terms of service. Of a total of 543 stated purposes (see 3.1.1.), only 53 purposes were obscured by the service provider. This is roughly 10%. The purpose of profiling the user in order to make a profit has the second highest rate of attempts to obscure the purposes with about 20% (13 out of 65) being obscured. This is not a surprise, because that purpose is probably the most sensitive usage of user data possible. Therefore users may very well be discontented if they find out about that usage. Hence, it makes a lot of sense for service providers to obscure this purpose. In contrast to that, the purpose of fulfilling legal obligations is never obscured. The fact that services use data in order to verify the users' age is obscured in 21% (9 out of 46) of the cases. Beneath the differences between the purposes, there are also differences between the various member states. While in Bulgaria 13 of 41 named purposes are obscured (32%), this is never the case in Denmark, Italy, the Netherlands, Spain, Slovakia and the United Kingdom. A relatively high rate of obscured purposes can also be found in Germany, where 17% (10 out of 58 named purposes) of the purposes were obscured. The situation in Romania and Poland was quite similar. In those member states, eleven of 42 purposes (26%), respectively nine of 41 purposes (22%) are obscured. Interestingly, this was more likely the case in the new member states (Bulgaria, Poland, and Romania) to a lesser degree in the Czech Republic with three out of 16 (19%) purposes being obscured. However, this can by no means be generalized. On the one hand, Slovakia (none of their named purposes are obscured) as a new member state does not fit into the scheme at all and on the other hand Germany has one of the highest rates of obscured purposes.

3.1.3 Hide-and-seek: The favorite game of UGC providers?

3.1.3.1 Explanation

In addition to 3.1.1. and 3.1.2, it is also of high interest to analyse where the UGC service provider "informs" the user about his purposes. Are the purposes clearly visible, or is the purpose rather buried and hidden in the privacy policy and therefore hardly discernible for the user.

Several answers were possible. Partners were asked to fill in a "1" if the answer applied to the certain UGC. If the answer did not apply to the UGC the column was to be left blank.

The answer to the question was to be found in the privacy policy or in the terms of service.

Categories:

a) Underline purpose by using headlines

b) Underline purpose by using boldface in running text
c) Underline of purpose by emphasising relevant parts through colour or underline in running text
d) Underline purpose by dividing privacy policy into several section (in contrast to one long running text)
e) Purpose mentioned just in running text
f) There is one running text but purpose is buried in sub item
g) Other
h) Comment

Explanation: Question three contains seven parts. Each part deals with one purpose. Other purposes that partners were asked for in question one of part two were not considered here, due to the variety of other purposes. A comparison to the other purposes that were almost always mentioned does not allow any valuable conclusions.

3.1.3.2 Results of examination

Doc. 5

Question 3 Part 1-7	Underline purpose by using headlines	Underline purpose by using boldface in running text	Underline of purpose by emphasising relevant parts through colour or underline in running text	Underline purpose by dividing privicy policy into several sections (in contrast to one long running tex	Purpose mentioned just in running text	There is one running text but purpose is burried in the subitem
Part 1: To profile the user with a view to make profit	13	7	0	39	19	6
Part 2: To fulfill legal obligations	10	8	1	46	29	3
Part 3: To contact users	7	9	1	51	26	5
Part 4: For statistical reasons	15	4	5	40	22	2
Part 5: To enable features on the website to function	8	7	0	61	27	4
Part 6: For transaction/ payments	6	8	1	21	8	1
Part 7: To enable search engines not affiliated with the provider to access information	6	2	2	11	7	1
	65	45	10	269	138	22

Doc. 6

Member state	Underline purpose by using headlines	Underline purpose by using boldface in running text	Underline of purpose by emphasising relevant parts through colour or underline in running text	Underline purpose by dividing privicy policy into several sections (in contrast to one long running te)	Purpose mentioned just in running text	There is one running text but purpose is burried in the subitem
Austria	0	0	0	0	9	0
Bulgaria	0	0	0	10	22	1
Czech Republic	0	0	0	3	8	4
Denmark	6	0	0	7	18	0
France	0	0	0	39	0	0
Germany	5	14	1	41	9	2
Italy	1	2	0		10	
Malta	0	0	0	0	0	0
Netherlands	3	0	0	14	9	3
Poland	6	2	0	3	18	11
Romania	0	0	1	38	0	0
Slovakia	11	5	0	10	6	1
Spain	16	10	1	23	18	0
UK	10	1	7	16	4	0
Internationals	7	11	0	65	7	0
	65	45	10	269	138	22

The answers to question three of part one were surprising in their clearness. There was a distinct scheme visible as to the distribution of the various means by which service providers point out the different purposes. The differences between the various purposes in the distribution of the various means are hardly visible.

The division of the privacy policy into several sections was most commonly used in general. This was also true as to every single purpose in the chart. The method of simply mentioning the purposes in the running text was used not nearly as often as the division into several sections, but still significantly more often than all the other means. Again, this was true for every single purpose. The division of the privacy policy is a compromise between some consumer-friendly actions and a light work load for the provider. Using this approach, helps users to identify the various purposes for which data are collected. On the other hand, it is not very cost- or work-intensive for the service provider. The second most important approach; the mentioning of the purposes in the running text is not consumer-friendly at all and reveals once more that providers tend to use the easiest possible methods. The other methods possible were used significantly less frequently, as they require much more work. The usage of headlines was not as common, but still used with respect to many purposes. Once more, this means was almost always the third most common method with all purposes. However, there are two exceptions; the purpose of transactions and payments and the purpose of contacting the user. With respect to those purposes, the means was used less than boldface. This general observation is also true to the fourth most common means, the usage of boldface in a running text. The same exceptions exist here as well. This means is the third most common with respect to the mentioned purposes. The least common methods used by the service providers to point out purposes are purposes mentioned in the running text but buried in sub item (22 of the purposes) and the usage of different colours, respectively the underlining of a specific purpose (10 purposes).

A differentiation between the different member states is not useful when also considering the various purposes. This is due to the fact that some of the purposes were only used once in a specific member state. Thus conclusions can hardly be drawn. What is possible, however, is to take a look at the distribution of the methods used among the different member states. Doing this, the individual purposes for which those methods are used in the various member states are not to be considered. It becomes obvious that, although the distribution is somewhat similar to the results when referring to the various purposes, there are some differences in usage between the different member states. First of all, the reason for the fact that the division in several sections is so dominant is that the method is used to an incredibly great extent in some member states. Moreover, in some of those member states, a great number of purposes were identified. In France, for instance, all 39 identified purposes are pointed out to the consumer by this means. In Romania, the means is used 38 times and only one other means is used once, resembling the situation in France. In Germany, there were also other means used, but this means predominates with 41 uses, similarly it is used 65 times with respect to international services. Those four member states already make up more than two thirds of the total number of uses of that specific means. In contrast to that, there are other member states, in which most purposes are mentioned in the running text without further hints. Significantly, this was the case in Bulgaria, where the means was used twice as much as the division into several sections. The same is true as to Czech Republic and Denmark as well. In Poland it was used even six times more often than the division into several sections and in Italy, it was the only means of significance. Furthermore, the differences in the distribution of the other means between the different member states are also quite remarkable. In Austria, Bulgaria, the Czech Republic, and Romania, headlines are not used, whereas this is the instrument to point out 50% of the purposes in Slovakia, 26% in the UK and 24% of the purposes in Spain. Similarly, sub items are only of greater significance in Poland where they are used for 28% of the purposes. In the Czech Republic this is the case with 27% of the purposes, but the value of this number is lesser, as there were only 15 total purposes pointed out in the member state. The number of purposes for which boldface is used is mainly compromised of purposes mentioned by German, Spanish and International services. The fact that Spanish and International services have a similar number is not surprising, as all Spanish services are internationally active as well. Furthermore, it is noticeable that a different font colour or underlining is mainly used in the United Kingdom (7 times in the UK and 3 times in all other member states combined). With respect to the United Kingdom, it can be said that it is one of the member states that almost all means are used relatively frequently. The dominance of a specific method is not as big as in many other member states. The most common method is not even used for 50% of the purposes identified in the specific member state (for comparison: France 100%, Romania 97% Internationals 72%, Germany 57%). This is also true for Spain (34%), Slovakia (33%) and the Netherlands (48%).

3.1.4 Differentiation between the different data

3.1.4.1 Explanation

With respect to analyzing the providers' policies, we decided not only to analyse for which purposes providers collect data in general. We also think that it makes sense to differentiate between the different data collected and processed. This is due to the fact that it may be reasonable to collect some data for a specific purpose but not so much to collect the same data for a different purpose. Also it may be reasonable to ask for information to further one purpose, but other data may not even be helpful to further that specific purpose. Therefore we decided that the following information provided by the users has to be looked at separately:

1. Contact information[1] (Part 1)
2. Date of birth (Part 2)
3. Name (Part 3)
4. Personal information[2] (Part 4)
5. Employment information (Part 5)
6. IP address (Part 6)
7. Further user generated content[3] (Part 7)
8. Other (Part 8)

Each of these aspects constitutes a separate question. Again, the research partners were asked to use the answers suggested above if possible (3.1.3.1.: a-h). We included some voluntary information in these as well. This is due to the fact that most services do not require users to upload pictures, for instance. However, if

[1] Includes E-Mail, Telephone number, IM screen name etc.

[2]This is to include religious beliefs, political opinion, family, relationship status, hobbies, etc.

[3] This is to include further published content such as texts/photos/videos published by the user.

services enable users to do so, it is still of interest what they do with that data. Nevertheless, we asked partners to point out which information is voluntary. To do so, a '1' was to be inserted in the column. The information was normally to be found during the process of signing up. All other information needed should be found in the privacy policy or in the terms of service.

Note: It was well possible that the privacy policy or the terms of service did not provide the information needed to fill out the entire question with its seven parts. This question should show whether UGC service providers give detailed information about which data they use for which purpose. As it is unlikely that the UGC service providers give very detailed explanation about their purposes it was possible that partners did not find much information to this question.

3.1.4.2 Results of examination

Doc. 7

Data	To profile the user with a view to make profit	To fulfill legal obligations	To contact users	For statistical reasons	In order to verify users' age	To enable features on the website to function	For transactions/ payments	To enable search engines not affiliated with the provider to access informatio
Contact information	17	17	75	16	1	29	7	3
Date of birth	15	13	0	10	24	13	1	0
Name	13	10	28	9	0	30	8	7
Personal information	23	0	10	12	2	29	0	6
Employment information	18	0	1	9	0	15	1	4
IP-Address	14	29	2	35	0	16	1	4
Further user generated content	19	0	3	8	0	26	0	7

A connection between the fact that some information is voluntary and the usage of that specific information is not visible. An exception to this observation is the purpose of fulfilling legal obligations. This is due to the nature of the purpose. If information has to be collected by the service in order to fulfil legal obligations, the information can hardly be voluntary. This is also true the other way around. If a specific data is voluntary, it can hardly be used in order to fulfil legal obligations. Examples of this are personal and employment information.

Regarding the usage of the different data, it immediately catches the viewer's eye that the usage of specific data for specific purposes varies significantly. Personal information, for instance, is the kind of data that is used for profiling users more frequently than any other data. This can hardly be a surprise as information such as hobbies and personal interests are valuable data, especially with respect to personalised advertising. Interestingly, all the other data are used for profiling users as well. Therefore, it is possible to say that profiling users with a view to make profit is one of the most important purposes with respect to the collection of data.

Also all different data are used for the purpose of enabling features on the service's website to function. This can be explained by the fact that all of the given data are somewhat linked to communication. Almost all of them can somehow be used for some kind of feature on a social network platform, for example. Other data that do not seem to fit into that scheme like IP addresses can be used for the technical foundation of a different feature.

On the one hand, it has been shown that some data are used for all purposes and that all data are used for some purposes. On the other hand, it is not surprising that some data are not used for some of the listed purposes. This is due to the fact that it would hardly make sense to use the specific data for a given purpose. For instance, personal information is not used for the fulfilment of legal obligations. This makes sense, as hobbies, religious beliefs etc. are data that are generally not required by the authorities. Also, there is no connection whatsoever between personal information and transactions/payments.

However, there are further types of data that are used for various purposes. Contact information is unsurprisingly used to contact the user in the first place, but it is also used for all other purposes, although the significance for the verification of age is quite limited. However it is worth noting that it is even used for third party search engine to some degree. The same phenomenon can be observed regarding other data as well. The date of birth is commonly used for various purposes except for those that do not have any connection to it at all. There is no use for the date of birth when trying to contact the user, for payments and for third party search engines. IP addresses are also used for various purposes, mainly to fulfil legal obligations, but also for statistical reasons.

3.1.5 Involving third parties in the processing of data

3.1.5.1 Explanation

Some service providers disclose collected data to third parties. In fact, this happens quite frequently. As previously stated, the users' consent can only be informed when they know what their data are collected for. Furthermore, it is also necessary for them to know who except for the provider is involved in the process. Information on this could also be found in the privacy policy and the terms of service. A ´1´ was to be inserted in the "Answer" column if there is any information existing on the third parties involved in the processing of data. In the "Comment" column partners were asked to describe the information that is given. If the privacy policy or the terms of service did not include any information on third parties involved in the processing of data, the column was to be left blank.

It is important to realize that the fact that a service gives information regarding this issue does not mean that those services allow third parties to access the user data. Some services mention third parties by informing the user that third parties are not involved at all.

3.1.5.2 Results of examination

Doc. 8

Member State	Information on third parties	No information regarding third parties
Austria	0	6
Bulgaria	7	3
Czech Republic	1	9
Denmark	3	5
France	6	2
Germany	12	2
Italy	7	2
Malta	0	1
Netherlands	7	3
Poland	6	0
Romania	8	1
Slovakia	7	5
Spain	10	0
United Kingdom	8	2
International	17	0
	99	41

The results of question five of part one revealed that most services (71% - 99 out of 140 services) do inform their users about the fact whether third parties play a role in the processing of their personal data or not. Nevertheless, the amount of services that do not provide any information on third parties is significant (29% - 41 out of 140 services). The role of third parties in the processing of personal data is a sensitive issue, and therefore it makes sense to inform the user about the service's policy regarding third parties. For that reason it is surprising that the number of services that do not do so is still high. The high number can be due to the fact that third parties are not involved in the processing of personal data on those services and therefore providers do not find it worth mentioning. But it can also be possible that providers do not want to inform the user about the involvement of third parties. Once again, the results did also reveal that there are big discrepancies between the different member states under scrutiny. There are some nations, in which all services that were under examination offer information regarding third parties. This is the case in Poland, Spain and with 17 international services.

In most member states the number of the services which offer information is high, but not at 100%. This can be observed in Germany (86%), the United Kingdom (80%) and Italy (78%), for instance. However, there are other member states in which no information (Austria) or hardly any information is given (Czech Republic, 10%). In a last group of nations, there are about as many services that give information as there are services that do not inform. Those member states are Denmark, where a small majority of services do not inform the users and Slovakia, where a small majority of services do inform the users.

3.2 Part 2: Consenting once – consenting forever? Possibilities of refusing or withdrawing consent

The examination of purposes UGC service providers are obtaining consent for from their users is only the first step of analysing how they deal with obtaining consent. Apart from that, it is inevitable to also focus on how they deal with users that are either not willing to grant their consent in the first place or who later wish to withdraw their initial consent for different reasons. It is also useful to look at whether the possibility exists for users to only give partial consent or whether they are forced to either consent to the privacy policy as a whole or refuse it altogether. Only by doing this, it is possible to gain information about the whole area of obtaining consent. Apart from the question of whether it is theoretically possible for users to withdraw or refuse their consent, one must also look at further key aspects such as the consequences that users have to bear if they decide not to grant consent or decide to withdraw it.

3.2.1 Is there a possibility of granting only partial consent?

3.2.1.1 Explanation

This criterion deals with the question whether users are forced to consent to the provider's entire privacy policy or whether he or she is able to agree to some parts and refuse others. The criterion is of immense significance, as it allows drawing a conclusion as to how free the user´s choice actually is. If they do not have the option of accepting only parts of the privacy policy, the policy might be regarded as dictated and the user may be 'forced' to consent by the provider. If the user has the chance to grant only partial consent, this option would probably come up in the initial process of consenting upon registration.Categories of possible answers:

a) User has to consent to the entire privacy policy
b) User has the opportunity to agree to some provisions and to refuse others
c) Comment

3.2.1.2 Results of examination

Doc. 9

Member State	User has to consent to the entire privacy policy	User has the opportunity to agree to some provisions and to refuse others	No consent required
Austria	5	1	0
Bulgaria	8	0	2
Czech Republic	8	0	2
Denmark	7	0	1
France	8	0	0
Germany	11	0	3
Italy	8	0	1
Malta	0	0	1
Netherlands	10	0	0
Poland	6	0	0
Romania	9	0	0
Slovakia	12	0	0
Spain	10	0	0
United Kingdom	10	0	0
International	14	2	1
	126	3	11

The results of the research regarding the possibility of a partial consent to the privacy policy were generally expected. However, the fact that only three out of 140 services (2%) allowed the users to partly refuse consent came as a surprise. It was expected that the vast majority would not allow the users to do so, but it was also thought that the share of those allowing the users to grant only partial consent would be significantly greater than it turned out to be. The assumption that most services would not grant this opportunity turned out to be correct with the overwhelming majority of 126 out of 140 services (90%) not allowing consumers to grant only partial consent. There can be numerous reasons for this prevalent approach. The most plausible explanations can be, firstly, the complex and costly process of saving various different consents from multitudinous users. It might be very difficult for the service provider to track during the usage of each user who consented to which purpose. Secondly, the possibility for the user of consenting only partially to the privacy policy is not in the interest of the service provider. By allowing partial consent the service provider runs the risk of not receiving users consent for personal advertisement or newsletters etc. which would be a financial disadvantge for the provider. The fact that eleven services (8%) did not require consent was surprising again. This is due to the fact that two of these eleven services did have a privacy policy, but did not require consent. Due to the clearness of the findings regarding this aspect and the evenness of the distribution of results, it is not necessary to distinguish between the different member states.

3.2.2 The consequences of not granting consent – The sink or swim approach

3.2.2.1 Explanation

In many services, the user is forced upon registration to accept the privacy policy. For instance, this is done by combining the mere process of signing up with granting consent. Thus, users are not able to gain access to the service without granting consent. However, there might be other service providers that let users access the service, although they have not given consent to the privacy policy. This difference can be of significance, because the latter gives users much more options other than refusing the privacy policy and not being able to use the network anymore or accepting a privacy policy they do not favour in order to be able to access the service. If consenting and signing up are linked to each other, the user will not be allowed to proceed with the registration unless he or she consents to the privacy policy. If there are any restrictions on the use of the service linked to not granting consent, he or she will most likely be informed about those at this point as well.

Categories of possible answers:

a) The user will not be allowed to use the service
b) The users will only be able to use parts of the service
c) The user will be able to use the service without facing any restrictions
d) Other
e) Comment

3.2.2.2 Results of examination

Doc. 10

Member State	Users will not be allowed to use the service	The users will only be able to use parts of the service	The users will be able to use the service without facing any restrictions	No consent required
Austria	5	0	1	0
Bulgaria	6	2	1	1
Czech Republic	8	0	0	2
Denmark	5	0	0	3
France	8	0	0	0
Germany	9	1	1	3
Italy	7	0	1	1
Malta	1	0	0	0
Netherlands	2	7	1	0
Poland	6	0	0	0
Romania	3	5	1	0
Slovakia	10	0	2	0
Spain	9	1	0	0
United Kingdom	10	0	0	0
International	15	0	1	1
	104	16	9	11

The results of the research as to the aspect of what consequences users would face for not granting consent do resemble those expected. Again, the number of services without a privacy policy and/or not requiring consent naturally remained stable (8% - eleven out of 140 UGC services). It was also not surprising that with 104 of 140 services (74%), the vast majority of services bans users not consenting to the privacy policy from using the service. Service provider use this consequence as a pressurising medium against the user. Users that want to participate in the UGC service have to decide whether they agree to the privacy policy or whether they are not able to use the serivce and do not have the possibility to interact with their friends. Because of the social pressure of not participating in something all the other friends do or of being left out many service providers exploit this situation in order to receive users consent of the user for all kind of purposes.

Nevertheless, 11% (16 out of 140 UGC services) of the services chose to only limit the user's ability to use the service. Finally, another group of services does not invoke any restrictions on users refusing consent at all (6% - 9 out of 140 UGC services). Interestingly, there are clear concentrations on various member states in those several categories. For instance, it catches the reader's eye that three quarters of the 16 services limiting access to the services are operating in the Netherlands (7) and Romania (5). With respect to the service providers that do not impose any restrictions on the user, it is interesting that two of those nine services operate in Slovakia.

3.2.3 Can users withdraw their initial consent?

3.2.3.1 Explanation

Along with the question of whether it is possible to grant only partial consent, it is also of interest to see whether it is possible for users to withdraw their initial consent. Users might accept the privacy policy for several reasons, including a lack of interest in the provisions or simply as a bargain in order to be able to use the service. For this, among other reasons, they may become dissatisfied with the privacy policy and may want to withdraw their consent. However, this may not always be possible. For example, some services do not delete shared content after accounts are cancelled. Thus, the original consent to display this content cannot be withdrawn. Other services might "force" the user to consent to the privacy policy in the process of registration, but later allow them to withdraw consent. This is a "Yes/No" question. If the user is able to withdraw his initial consent please write down a "1". If the user cannot withdraw his initial consent leave the column blank.

3.2.3.2 Results of examination

Doc. 11

Member State	Withdrawal possible	Other (no withdrawal possible, no information regarding withdrawal, no consent in first place required)
Austria	6	0
Bulgaria	6	4
Czech Republic	1	9
Denmark	3	5
France	0	8
Germany	5	9
Italy	5	4
Malta	1	0
Netherlands	4	6
Poland	6	0
Romania	7	2
Slovakia	5	7
Spain	0	10
United Kingdom	0	10
International	3	14
	52	88

Dealing with the withdrawal of consent, several difficulties arose. From the beginning, it was hard to predict what the results would look like here. Of the 140 services under scrutiny, only 52 (37%) explicitly allowed users to withdraw their initial consent. However, the problem with this aspect is mainly that it could not always be determined what the situation regarding the other 63% (88 out of 140 UGC services) of the services was. While it is clear with some of these services that no withdrawal is possible, other services do not offer any information regarding a possible withdrawal, thus making it impossible for researchers and for customers to find out whether they have a right to withdraw their consent. Some services do, for instance, allow users to delete the respective account, but do not state what happens with the stored data related to the account and possible licences related to the UGC linked to the account. Naturally, there are also those services that do not require any consent in the first place.
However, it is interesting, that there are notable differences among the member states when looking at this aspect of the research. In Austria and Poland, for instance, a withdrawal of consent is possible with all services and in Romania it was possible with 78% (7 out of 9 Romanian UGC services), whereas the situation is quite to the contrary in France, Spain and the UK. Here none of the services under scrutiny clearly allow a complete withdrawal of consent. Similarly, in the Czech Republic 90% (9 out of 10 UGC services) of the services do not provide this option. The situation in Bulgaria, Denmark, Germany, Italy, the Netherlands and Slovakia is relatively balanced. It is interesting to see that in four out of five new member states with the exception of the Czech Republic, the situation is either balanced or in favour of the right of withdrawal. This is not the case with the majority of internationally operating services (only 3 of 17). With respect to that, one also needs to consider that most services under scrutiny in Spain and the UK do also operate internationally.

3.2.4 Is partial withdrawal possible? If so, to which extent can users withdraw consent?

3.2.4.1 Explanation

When browsing several UGC services, we noticed that some of them allow users to grant only partial consent. Nevertheless, some of the services that do not do so allow users to partially withdraw their consent afterwards. Information on this was usually to be found in the privacy settings or the terms of service. The two suggested answers in the list (a and b) we came across quite often in our preliminary research. Partners were asked to name other areas in which consent may be withdrawn. If partial withdrawal is impossible, partners should have left the answer sheet blank.

Categories of possible answers:

a) Promotional e-mail delivered by the provider

b) Personalized ads

c) Other

d) Comment

3.2.4.2 Results of examination

Doc. 12

Member State	Promotional e-mail delivered by the provider	Personalized ads	Other	Partial withdrawal not possible
Austria	0	0	0	6
Bulgaria	4	0	2	4
Czech Republic	2	1	1	7
Denmark	2	4	1	2
France	7	2	0	1
Germany	4	5	3	8
Italy	3	0	0	6
Malta	0	0	0	1
Netherlands	7	6	2	3
Poland	0	0	0	6
Romania	5	1	2	2
Slovakia	1	0	1	10
Spain	7	10	0	0
United Kingdom	3	2	0	6
International	7	6	4	4
	52	37	16	66

As suspected, it was found out that the options of withdrawing consent with respect to the delivery of promotional e-mails and personalized ads were prevalent. Of 140 services, 52 (37%) allow users to withdraw their consent regarding the delivery of promotional e-mails. This is mainly the case in France, the Netherlands, Romania, and Spain and with the international services. This does not mean that those options do not exist in other member states, but in the listed ones, the share is especially noteworthy. The amount of services enabling users to withdraw consent regarding personalized advertisements is lesser, but with 37 services (26%) still of high significance. This is the case quite often in the Netherlands, Spain, with international services and with some significance in Germany and Denmark. It is interesting that many services tend to allow users to withdraw consent with respect to both listed aspects. Thus, the relatively high numbers for those two categories are based on a relatively small number of services allowing both (see the Netherlands and Spain), with many other services allowing neither the one nor the other. Numerous services also allow users to withdraw their consent concerning other aspects as well. Some of those services do not really offer an option to explicitly withdraw consent, but instead allow users to delete any content ever published on the service by the user including his or her e-mail address. Also, some - particularly German - services allow users to withdraw their consent regarding the use of cookies and web beacons by the service. Users of some other services are also able to withdraw their consent regarding the transfer of their personal data to third parties. One UGC service provider also allows users to contact the service and directly state which usage of the data originally transferred to the service should be terminated and what kind of data should be included in the withdrawal. Thus, the user can decide in detail what he wants the provider to be able to do. In contrast to the services just described, the majority of 66 (out of 140) services (47%) do not allow users to withdraw any consent. When dealing with this data, it is important to also consider the results of part two regarding the purposes for which data are collected. If a service does not use personalized advertisements, naturally the service will not enable users to withdraw consent, as users have never agreed to such proceedings. However, the results acquired here, are sufficient for a broad overview over the options given to consumers concerning the partial withdrawal of consent. The last scenario, the case where users are not able to withdraw consent can be observed quite well in Slovakia, Poland, the Czech Republic and Italy. In those member states, the vast majority of services do not allow users to withdraw consent. This is also noticeable to some extent in Germany. But again, it is necessary to consider that this may be due to the fact that some services do not even require consent in the first place. Nevertheless, the reason that partial withdrawal is not possible can be also due to other factors. As already stated in 3.2.2.2 service providers are not interested in partial consent and respectively partial withdrawal. However, it is quite the contrary because partial withdrawal leads such as partial consent to the fact that service provider loose a financial main pillar. It is clear that users would use the opportunity of partial withdrawal to withdraw promotional e-mails as well as personalized advertisement. By not providing such tool service providers do not run the risk of losing money.

3.2.5 After the withdrawal...

3.2.5.1 Explanation

This question is also closely related to the previous ones. It is important for the same reasons, as is 3.2.2., since the only difference is that question 3.2.2. deals with the initial refusal of consent and question 3.2.5. deals with the later withdrawal of consent. If users have the right to withdraw their initial consent, it is of importance to find out what kind of consequences they face if they do withdraw consent, as those consequences might deter users from taking this step. Consequences such as not receiving promotional e-mails anymore after withdrawing consent were not to be listed here. Hints at the answers to this question were found either in the privacy policy or the terms of service. If consent could be withdrawn on the website, partners were asked to pay attention to possible pop up boxes, informing the user of the consequences.

Categories of possible answers:

a) Users will be excluded from the service or have to delete their account.
b) There will be some restrictions on using the service
c) Users will not face any consequences at all
d) Other
e) Comment

3.2.5.2 Results of examination

Doc. 13

Member State	Users will be excluded or will have to delete their account	There will be some restrictions on using the service	Users will not face any consequences at all	Other (e.g. no information given, no withdrawal possible, no consent was required in first place)
Austria	6	0	0	0
Bulgaria	2	4	1	3
Czech Republic	8	0	0	2
Denmark	3	4	0	1
France	8	0	0	0
Germany	3	1	1	9
Italy	3	0	0	6
Malta	1	0	0	0
Netherlands	4	6	0	0
Poland	6	0	0	0
Romania	4	3	0	2
Slovakia	4	0	1	7
Spain	0	3	7	0
United Kingdom	10	0	0	0
International	8	2	4	3
	70	23	14	33

The consequences of a complete withdrawal vary among the different UGC services. Nevertheless, there is a clear tendency toward a forced cancellation/deletion of the account if consent is withdrawn. The following numbers will not include those services that do not require consent, do not have a privacy policy, respectively do not allow a withdrawal of consent or do not give any information regarding these issues at all. Those services make up 24% (33 out of 140 UGC services) of all services. The reason for not considering them when analysing this aspect is that the objective of this criterion is to only examine the consequences that users face after withdrawing consent if that is possible. Therefore only 107 services were to be included in this part. Of these 107 services, 70 services (65%) will exclude users from the service or force them to delete their accounts in the case of a withdrawal of consent. Again this consequence can be seen - as already stated in 3.2.2.2 - as a pressurising medium used by the service provider. If a user withdraws his or her consent he or she should no longer be able to use the service. In such a situation the user should really reconsider his decision of withdrawing his personal data. On the other hand, this consequence can also be only the implementation of legal requirements in some member states. 14 out of 107 services (13%) do not impose any consequences on the users for withdrawing consent. Interestingly, seven of those services operate in Spain and four of them are categorised as international UGC service providers. This may indicate that the international providers tend to offer users the possibility of at least partially withdrawing their consent, and for that purpose do not impose any consequences on users for withdrawing. The numbers for Spain do also support this assumption, as the services under review in Spain are all internationally operating. Important to notice is that many of those services only waive consequences when consent is only withdrawn partially. Apart from that, there were also 23 (out of 107) services (22%) that imposed some restrictions on using the service. Those services were mainly concentrated in Bulgaria (4), Denmark (4), the Netherlands (6), Romania (3) and Spain (3). Looking at those results, a pattern cannot be found.

It is quite interesting to take note of the various consequences that UGC service providers impose on users. The two Bulgarian UGC services *Sibir.bg* and *Elmaz.com*, for example, let users still see smaller versions of photos provided by other users, but the full version will not be available anymore. Other services like *VBox 7* will basically cancel the user's account as to the user's ability to upload user generated content, however the user will retain his right to access the content provided by other users. The Bulgarian UGC service *BG-Mama* on the other hand, will still allow users to read articles and to see other users´ opinions in the forums, profiles and pictures. Another interesting, but somewhat self-evident consequence is that once consent as to the use of the user's email is withdrawn, the user will not be able to obtain his or her password if it is forgotten.

3.2.6 Hide-and-seek again: How is the user informed about his right to withdraw consent?

3.2.6.1 Explanation

Even if users do have the right to withdraw their consent, it makes a huge difference how they are informed of this possibility. One can think of various means of doing so. With some of these methods, users may hardly take notice of their right. Other means may enable users to realise more easily that they can withdraw consent, thus enabling them to make use of this option. This aspect is worth taking a closer look at, as it is also related to the process of granting/withdrawing consent. The right to withdraw consent will hardly benefit users, if they are not aware of it.

Categories of possible answers:

a) The user is informed about this in the privacy policy
b) The user is informed about this in the terms of service
c) There is a hint at this possibility in the privacy setting part of the service
d) There is no information about a withdrawal
e) Other
f) Comment

3.2.6.2 Results of examination

Doc. 14

Member State	The user is informed about this in the privacy policy	The user is informed about this in the terms of service	There is a hint at this possibility in the privacy setting part of the service	There is no information about a withdrawal	Other (no specific consent required)
Austria	2	4	0	0	0
Bulgaria	1	1	0	6	2
Czech Republic	0	1	0	7	2
Denmark	0	3	3	2	0
France	2	5	0	1	0
Germany	7	2	0	2	4
Italy	4	2	0	2	1
Malta	0	0	1	0	0
Netherlands	3	0	0	7	0
Poland	4	6	0	0	0
Romania	5	5	0	2	0
Slovakia	0	2	0	7	3
Spain	10	0	0	0	0
United Kingdom	0	9	0	1	0
International	8	0	4	5	2
	46	40	8	42	14

With question 3.2.6, it was possible that more than one response was accurate. This is due to the fact that service providers may very well inform the users about their right to withdraw consent by using various means. The results of this part of the examination show how great the share of services is that do not give any information regarding a possible withdrawal. This is the case with 42 out of 140 of the services (30%), notably in the Czech, Republic, the Netherlands and Slovakia (7 each). International services account for 5 of those and the remaining services are distributed relatively easily among the different member states. The lack of information about a withdrawal can be due to different reasons. One very plausible reason can be related to the fact that service providers are not interested in a withdrawal of an initial consent. Service providers try to avoid encouraging users' awareness of the possibility of withdrawing their personal data.

However, the majority of services do inform the user mainly using provisions in the privacy policy (33% - 46 out of 140 services) or the terms of service (29% - 40 out of 140 services). Especially regarding those two methods, there are substantial differences among the various member states. While international services, for instance, tend to use the privacy policy (47% - 8 out of 17 international services) instead of the terms of service (0), in the UK the terms of service (9 out of 10 analysed services) prevail over the privacy policy (0). In Spain and Germany, the privacy policy is also clearly prevailing, whereas in Denmark and France, the terms of service are more frequently used than the privacy policy. A relatively small share of the services give a hint at the possibility of withdrawing consent in the privacy settings (6% - 8 out of 140 services). This method is mainly used by international providers (4) and in Denmark (3).

3.2.7 Do the privacy policy or the terms of service inform the user about the consequences for his or her generated content after deleting the account?

3.2.7.1 Explanation

Once the user deletes his or her account it is of high interest what happens to his or her generated content. Is it also deleted, partially deleted, or is it still available on the UGC service? For this reason we asked whether the privacy policy or the terms of service mention anything about the disposition of generated content after the deletion of the user´s account. This was a "yes" or "no" answer. If the privacy policy or the terms of service mention anything about the disposition of the generated content after the user deleted his or her account partners were asked to fill in a "1". If there is no information at all, the column was to be left blank.

Categories:

Yes = fill in a 1 in the column

No = leave the column blank

3.2.7.2 Results of examination

Doc. 15

Member State	Yes	Do not provide any information
Austria	6	0
Bulgaria	4	6
Czech Republic	2	8
Denmark	3	5
France	2	6
Germany	8	6
Italy	3	6
Malta	0	1
Netherlands	2	8
Poland	3	3
Romania	3	6
Slovakia	4	8
Spain	9	1
United Kingdom	4	6
International	7	10
	60	80

Surprisingly, the majority of services do not inform the users of the impact the deletion of accounts will have on the saved data (57% - 80 out of 140 services). Only 43% (60 out of 140) of the services state either in the terms of service or in the privacy policy what those consequences could possibly look like. It is quite compelling that 90% of the services under scrutiny in Spain do so, but only 20% of those in the Czech Republic and the Netherlands. In many member states the share is between 33% and 50% (International, UK, Slovakia, Romania, Italy, Bulgaria etc.) An exception is also Germany, with 62% giving some information in the terms of service.

3.2.8 How does the process of withdrawing consent work technically?

3.2.8.1 Explanation

With regard to withdrawing consent, one should also look at how the process of withdrawing works in practice. The means by which this is carried out are likely to affect the users' choice as to whether they want to make use of their ability to withdraw consent. If the process is quite complicated or costly, users might feel discouraged to withdraw consent. This is even more the case if costs like sending letters etc. are linked to withdrawing consent. If the user can only withdraw consent by deleting his account, the correct answer depends on how the user can do so. If, for instance, an e-mail is required to delete the account, a) would be the correct answer.

Categories of possible answers:

a) An e-mail can be sent to the service provider
b) A letter can be sent to the service provider
c) The process can be completed on the service's website
d) Other
e) Comment

Note: Several answers were possible!

3.2.8.2 Results of examination

Doc. 16

Member State	An e-mail can be sent to the service provider	A letter can be sent to the service provider	The process can be completed on the service's website	Other	No information given; no withdrawal possible
Austria	4	1	4	0	0
Bulgaria	2	0	5	0	3
Czech Republic	2	1	4	0	5
Denmark	4	1	4	0	1
France	4	3	2	0	0
Germany	5	4	4	0	6
Italy	3	2	1	1	4
Malta	0	0	1	0	0
Netherlands	9	5	4	0	0
Poland	3	0	6	0	0
Romania	6	5	2	0	2
Slovakia	0	1	6	0	6
Spain	1	0	9	0	1
United Kingdom	10	3	7	0	0
International	1	0	13	1	3
	54	26	72	2	31

Considering the results of the examination regarding question eight of part two, it catches the viewer's eye that many services offer users various possibilities to withdraw consent, which may make it easier for users to actually make use of their right to withdraw consent. This phenomenon could be observed quite often in Austria, the Netherlands, Romania and the UK. This is also noticeable to some degree in Germany and Poland as well. Generally, it does not seem to be surprising that many services do actually allow users to withdraw consent on the service's website. This is possible with 72 out of 140 services (51%). Enabling the user to do so seems rather useful, as the internet and the service's website is generally used by the consumer. Therefore, it is normally quite convenient for the user to also be able to withdraw his or her consent on the website itself. In addition to that the feature of withdrawing consent on the service´s website is for the service provider itself an easy and inexpensive way to complete his duty of providing a withdrawal function. Features such as letters or other forms of communication are more expensive and time-consuming. Furthermore, the advantage of withdrawing consent on the service´s website is that there does not arise a media discontinuity. This is virtually the only method used by international services with 13 of the 17 under scrutiny doing this. The situation is quite similar in Bulgaria, Poland, Slovakia and Spain where the vast majority of services tend to use this method. 54 out of 140 services (39%) also allow users to withdraw consent by sending an e-mail to the provider. This has the same advantages as the previously discussed method, as it is almost as convenient for someone who frequently uses the internet. This method is of special significance in the UK and the Netherlands where it is offered even more frequently than the option of withdrawing consent on the website itself. Interestingly, 26 out of 140 services (19%) also allow users to withdraw consent in written form by sending a letter. At first sight, this seems rather surprising, as consent is normally obtained online. However, this may be due to several reasons, one of them being legal requirements in the specific member states. Furthermore, using this method, the withdrawal could possibly be proven more easily before court and it also enables the withdrawal of consent when internet access is not available for whatever reason. All the same this method is very costly and time-consuming. Because of that reason the percentage is not very high. Again, there is a division between the various member states. While this method is not uncommon in Germany, Romania, the Netherlands, France and to a lesser degree in the UK, it is virtually not used in the other member states. In Bulgaria, Poland, and Spain and with international providers, this option does not exist at all.

3.2.9 Changing the privacy policy – changing consent?

3.2.9.1 Explanation

Parallel to the questions aiming at the consequences of not granting, or withdrawing the initial consent, this question deals with the consequences of not accepting changes to the privacy policy. Those consequences might affect the users' decisions as well. The user may receive information on the consequences when he is informed of the changes. However, this is not likely to happen during the research process. For information on the possible consequences, partners were asked to check the privacy policy and the terms of service. If no information was to be found in the privacy policy or in the terms of service, partners were asked to contact the UGC service provider and ask how he deals with the question.

Categories of possible answers:

a) The user is no longer able/allowed to use the service
b) The old privacy policy will remain in effect with respect to the particular user

c) Other
d) Comment

3.2.9.2 Results of examination

Doc. 17

Member State	The user is no longer able/allowed to use the service	The old privacy policy will remain in effect with respect to the particular user	Other
Austria	6	0	0
Bulgaria	4	0	6
Czech Republic	8	0	2
Denmark	5	0	3
France	7	1	0
Germany	5	1	8
Italy	5	0	4
Malta	1	0	0
Netherlands	4	0	0
Poland	6	0	0
Romania	7	0	2
Slovakia	2	1	9
Spain	8	1	1
United Kingdom	10	0	0
International	10		7
	88	4	42

With respect to the last aspect of part three, it is quite astonishing that a great number of services do not give any information as to the consequences of a withdrawal. One would assume that this is necessary for users in order to make an educated decision about the issue of withdrawal. Such information was mainly missing with many of the international services. Nevertheless, there were some hints implicating that users will have to delete their accounts. Apart from this, there were some other interesting approaches used, for instance in Slovakia. Five of the services under scrutiny in Slovakia had regulations enabling them to pretend that the user agreed to the changes immediately. This construction is somewhat forcing users to delete their accounts if they disagree, so there is a similarity to the approach many other services use. However, by this time, the user has already "accepted" the changes according to the construction used. These and other methods ("Other") were used with 31% (42 out of 135 services) of the services, this number including services not enabling users to withdraw consent and services not requiring consent in the first place. In spite of the methods used here, 88 of 135 services (65%) force the user to delete his or her account if there is a disagreement regarding the new policy. A tiny majority of 4 services (3%) of the services allow users to continue the use of the service under the regulations used previously. Looking at the various member states, there are no further significant differences among them that could not be easily explained by the fact that in some member states, there were numerous services under scrutiny without any privacy regulations at all or not requiring consent.

3.3 Part 3: Policies and technical features used for obtaining consent

3.3.1 "Accept privacy policy" – print now?

3.3.1.1 Explanation

When using the internet, users can never be certain that the content that is available online will remain available. Thus, it may make sense for the user to save a copy of the privacy policy or to print it out. This will give the user the ability to know the exact terms he or she consented to at a later stage. This can be of extraordinary significance in the case where a UGC provider changes his privacy policy without the user's consent. Where such a feature is not available, the user is of course able to simply copy and paste the privacy policy. However, a much higher amount of work is necessary. This might very well keep users from obtaining a copy of the privacy policy. Presumably, the user will not even remember to save or copy the privacy policy he or she consented to. Thus this question is aiming at the possibility of offering a direct link enabling the user to print the document or save a copy. Furthermore, the mere fact that a separate link to print or save the document exists may increase the user‘s desire to actually read the document, as it may seem more significant to him as a result.

Categories of possible answers:

a) The privacy policy is only displayed on the website
b) There is a hyperlink directing the user to a print version of the document
c) The service offers a document the user can save
d) Other
e) Comments

Example of b):

Doc. 18

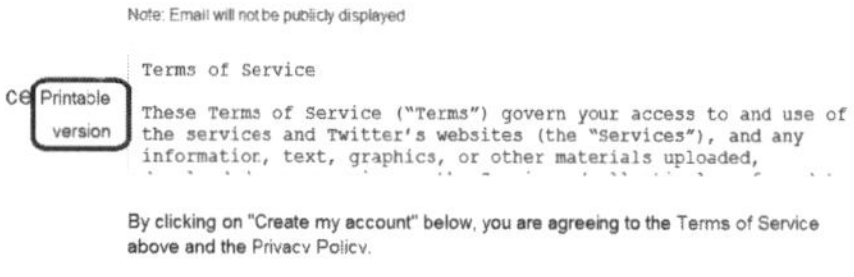

A UGC service was only to be categorized here if the link to the printable version is not hidden on the website and easy to find. (For comparison: see 3.3.4.)

Example of c):

In this category, an option to download a file is sufficient. However, the link must be placed as stated in b).

Explanation of d) and e)

The WWU established two other categories. The partners were requested to use the "Other" column whenever none of the stated possibilities applied to the analysed UGC service and to explain how the provider deals with the certain question. In addition to that, the "Comment" column was created for any additional comment or explanation regarding one of the answers listed. The partners were also asked to proceed in the same way in the following questions.

3.3.1.2 Results of examination

Doc. 19

Member State	The privacy policy is only displayed on the website	There is a hyperlink directing the user to a print version of the document	The service offers a document the user can save	No privacy policy nor terms of service	Other
Austria	3	3	3	0	0
Bulgaria	9	0	0	1	0
Czech Republic	7	1	1	2	0
Denmark	8	0	0	0	0
France	6	1	1	0	0
Germany	7	5	1	2	0
Italy	7	0	0	2	0
Malta	0	0	0	1	0
Netherlands	8	1	0	1	0
Poland	5	1	1	0	0
Romania	8	1	1	0	0
Slovakia	12	0	0	0	0
Spain	9	1	0	0	0
United Kingdom	9	1	0	0	0
International	16	1	1	0	0
	114	16	9	9	0

The examination has clearly shown that with the vast majority of UGC services the privacy policy is only available on the website. This was in fact the case with 114 of a total of 140 services (81%) in this particular issue. Only a small number of services offered a printable version (11% - 16 out of 140 services) or a link to download the file (6% - 9 out of 140 services). While this part of the result is not particularily surprising, it is worth noting, however, that nine out of 140 services (6%) did not provide any privacy policy at all. This is quite remarkable, as there are no regulations of these UGC sites as to the processing of user generated content, although this is the purpose of those services. Services without any visible privacy policy have been detected in Germany (*spickmich.de* and *exika.de*), the Czech Republic (*Česko-slovenská filmová databáze.cz* and *Gamepark.cz*) and Italy (*diggita.com* and *meemi.com)* and once each in Bulgaria (*Edno23)*, Malta (*Skola Ħbieb*) and the Netherlands (*zoover*). Some of these services only refer to a Creative Commons License. The content that users submit is therefore subject to that license. Other services, however, do not have any regulations regading privacy or only provide a small Frequently Asked Questions (FAQ) section. In contrast to that, there are services that offer even further advice to the user, such as instruction videos. Some providers only allow users to view the privacy policy during the process of registration, but do not allow users to view it afterwards. Both services that do so are Slovakian (*sexifotky.sk* and *spoluziaci.sk*). All 17 internationally operating providers that were subject to this research do have a privacy policy, however all of them only display it on the website. The only exception to this is Xing which also offers a download and a link to print the policy immediately. Worth mentioning in this context is the fact that some UGC services may superficially appear to offer the user a printable version of the privacy policy. However, this feature is in fact not working due to bad programming or internal errors (Austria - *szene1.at* and *secondlife.com*) or not accessible (Bulgaria - *contacto*).

There are several possible reasons for these results. First of all, it is significantly easier for a provider to only display the privacy policy on the website. Providing a printable version requires no work. Although this work load can easily be handled by average UGC service providers, providers do hardly have any interest in creating such features. There are no advantages for the provider if users keep a copy of the privacy policy they consented to. Moreover, the positive effect on consumers is rather small as well, as only a tiny minority of users would actually make use of such an option. Interestingly, these features can mainly be found on the websites of German or Austrian UGC services. This can possibly be explained by the legal requirements in these countries.

3.3.2 Technical features used for obtaining consent

3.3.2.1 Explanation

Especially regarding technical features for obtaining, UGC service providers use very different approaches. The user formally registers by clicking a ‘register’ or ‘sign up’ button. With some services (e.g. *Facebook.com*), clicking this button includes accepting the terms of service and the provider’s privacy policy. However, other providers use a previously checked box, which the user has to uncheck in order to refuse consent. This method is called `opt-out´. Unless the user actively unchecks the box, he or she consents. Moreover, there is another significant approach, also using a checkbox. With that approach, the user has to check the blank checkbox in order to grant consent and then click register. This approach is called ‘opt-in’.

This particular question is of great significance as it may influence the users’ awareness of consenting to the privacy policy extremely. It is possible that by only having to click the ‘register’ button, users may hardly realise that they are actually consenting to some kind of privacy policy. Furthermore, even if users are aware of doing so, this method might make giving consent seem quite trivial and of little or no importance. In contrast to this, using a pre-checked box seems likely to raise some awareness of the fact that users are consenting by clicking register. Nevertheless, giving consent may still appear to be insignificant and trivial. Users might feel discouraged from refusing consent. Unlike the other alternatives, the opt-in process seems to be much more likely to raise the user´s awareness to the process of giving consent, and by actively having to check the box; it might make consenting appear more significant and valuable to the users.

Categories of possible answers:

a) Consent is implied by clicking the ‘register´ button
b) The checkbox is blank, the user has to check it
c) A pre-checked checkbox is used
d) Other
e) Comment

Example of a)

Doc. 20

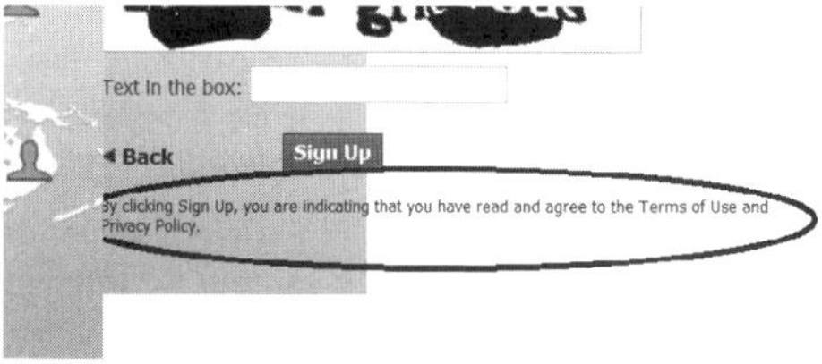

Example of b):

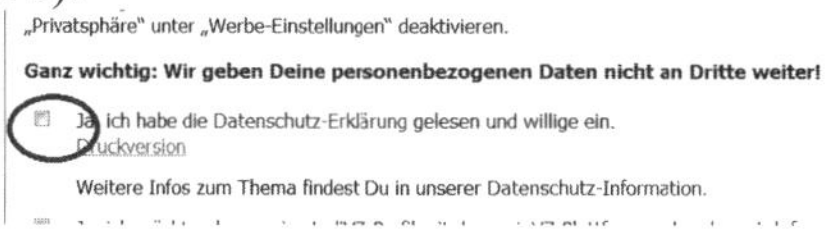

Example of c):

Same as b), but box would be pre-checked.

3.3.2.2 Results of examination

Doc. 21

Member State	Consent is implied by clicking the 'register' button	The checkbox is blank, the user has to check it	A pre-checked checkbox is used	No consent is asked during the registration process
Austria	1	4	0	1
Bulgaria	4	5	0	1
Czech Republic	1	7	0	2
Denmark	7	1	0	0
France	1	4	1	2
Germany	3	7	0	4
Italy	3	3	2	1
Malta	1	0	0	0
Netherlands	2	7	1	0
Poland	1	4	0	1
Romania	2	4	1	2
Slovakia	11	1	0	0
Spain	6	4	0	0
United Kingdom	5	4	0	1
International	13	3	0	1
	61	58	5	16

As one can clearly see in the chart above, most service providers either imply consent in clicking "register" (44% - 61 out of 140 services) or offer a blank checkbox that the user has to check and then click "sign up" in order to grant his or her consent and to use the service (41% - 58 out of 140 services). While internationally active providers tend to use the first option of implied consent (76% - 13 out of all 17 international services), there are some member states in which this means of obtaining consent also predominates (Slovakia: 92%, Denmark: 88%). In contrast to that, there are also various member states in which the usage of a blank check box is common (Netherlands: 70%, Czech Republic: 70%, Germany: 50%). However, there are also other member states in which the two dominant methods are equally used. This is the case, for example, in the UK or Italy. Only a small minority of services use a pre-checked checkbox (4% - 5 out of 140 services). This is the case with two providers in Italy (*me2.it* and *theclub.it)* and one each in France (*Le Guide)*, the Netherlands (*Relatieplanet*) and Romania (*sentimente.ro*). Similar to the previous criterion, it is again surprising that 16 out of 140 service providers do not require any consent at all during the registration process (11%). Obviously, the providers that do not have a privacy policy cannot ask for consent, as there is nothing for the user to consent to. Nevertheless, there are some providers that do not ask for consent, but actually do have a privacy policy. This catches the readers' eyes, as one would assume that a privacy policy does not make sense, if users do not consent to it.

It is not a surprise that many services imply consent in clicking the "sign up" button. This is due to the fact that this means is capable of detracting users' attention from the fact that they are agreeing to a privacy policy, thus gaining critical users, who would not grant otherwise. A blank check box is used about as much. This method, in contrast, represents a different approach. While users are still not likely to actually read the privacy policy, they have a better chance to know that they are giving consent. Therefore, they also have a better chance to read the necessary information for an informed consent in the privacy policy. Hence, this means is more consumer friendly than the previously discussed one. The distribution of the various means among the member states may be related to the legal situation in the respective states once again. The fact that international services are much more apt to use the first method is likely to be related to the matter of fact that most of those services originate in North America, where consumer protection law is not as strict as in Europe. Also privacy does not have the same importance in public sentiment in North America.

3.3.3 Privacy policy and the terms of service – one document?

3.3.3.1 Explanation

This criterion deals with the question of whether the privacy policy of a UGC service is included in the terms of service or whether the privacy policy is a separate document. This question is of great importance. Privacy policies that are part of the terms of service are usually hidden and not very obvious to the user. Often the user is not aware of the fact that by consenting to the terms of service he or she is simultaneously agreeing to the privacy policy as well, unless he or she actually reads the terms of services entirely. In contrast, privacy policies that are completely separated from the terms of services and that stand next to the terms of services are much more visible to the user. In this case, the privacy policy catches the attention of the user more effectively and he or she can consent more consciously.

Categories of possible answers:

a) Privacy policy is included in the terms of service
b) Privacy policy is a separate document
c) Comment

Note: A privacy policy is said to be included in terms of service, if regulations regarding privacy can be found in it and there is no explicit privacy policy apart from that. Furthermore, this is to be assumed whenever the privacy policy is only accessible using a hyperlink provided in the terms of service.

3.3.3.2 Results of examination

Doc. 22

Member State	Privacy policy is included in the terms of service	Privacy policy is a seperate document	No privacy policy nor terms of service
Austria	1	5	0
Bulgaria	8	1	1
Czech Republic	7	1	2
Denmark	5	3	0
France	4	4	0
Germany	0	11	3
Italy	1	6	2
Malta	0	0	1
Netherlands	2	8	0
Poland	2	4	0
Romania	3	6	0
Slovakia	8	4	0
Spain	2	8	0
United Kingdom	0	10	0
International	0	17	0
	43	88	9

The fact that there are some services that do not have a privacy policy need not be discussed any further. As one would expect, the majority of privacy regulations were actually segregated from the terms of service or other documents (63% - 88 out of 140 services). Nevertheless, the amount of services that use terms of service which also regulate privacy issues is of some significance. This was the case with 31% (43 out of 140) of the services under scrutiny, whereas only 6% did not have a privacy policy at all. Once again, it is interesting to compare the results in the various member states. In fact, all 17 internationally active services segregate the privacy policy from the terms of service or other related documents. The same situation can be found in the United Kingdom, where all ten selected providers segregated the policy from the terms of service. In Germany not all UGC services under scrutiny have a privacy policy but all of those that do have one separated their policy from the terms of service. In Spain 80 % (8 out of 10 services) did so as well. In contrast to this clear approach toward segregated privacy policies, the situation varies greatly when looking at other member states. In Romania and Poland for example, two thirds of the services have separate privacy policies. In Bulgaria, however, 80% (8 out of 10 services) of the services that do have privacy regulations integrated the privacy policy into their terms of service. Similar results can be found in the Czech Republic (70% - 7 out of 10), Slovakia (67% - 8 out of 12), Denmark (63% - 5 out of 8) and France (50% - 4 out of 8). According to these figures, integrated privacy policies appear to be more common with UGC services operating in the new member states, although this approach is also prevailing in Denmark and France.

Explanations for the means used by service providers, and the distribution of those means among the various member states are likely similar to the explanations for the results of other questions. Once again, legal requirements may lead the majority of UGC services to segregate the privacy policy from the terms of service. Doing so raises the awareness of consumers to the fact that a privacy policy exists. Dividing the regulations in the terms of service and the privacy policy also helps to improve their comprehensibility. On the other hand, not segregating has many advantages for the service providers, as it may help to overcome consumers' resistance if they do not realise that there are also privacy regulations to which they consent. This many lead to more users and thus to an increase in income, possibly through advertising. The fact that the consumer-friendly segregation is not used as much in the new member states as in the old ones may possibly be related to missing consumer protection laws or an ineffective enforcement of existing laws.

3.3.4 Hidden consent – the presentation of the privacy policy

3.3.4.1 Explanation

This criterion is related to the question as to whether the privacy policy is included in the terms of service (3.3.3) and to the question regarding technical features used by providers (3.3.2). Nevertheless, it is deemed necessary to establish this further criterion, as it allows a much broader approach to the question of how clearly the request for consent is presented to users. For example, with regard to 3.3.2, there may be some UGC services that do not even provide a check box. The user is only informed that by clicking 'register', he or she also accepts the privacy policy. However the lone use of criterion 3.3.2, does not allow an examination as to how obvious this fact is pointed out. This information could be quite obvious and well visible, but it could also be hidden and consist of fine print. Neither can criterion 3.3.3 provide broad answers to this question, as it only focuses on the question of whether the UGC's privacy policy is included in the terms of service or not. The significance of the issue whether the user is aware of giving consent need not be discussed any further, as this has been previously done (See 3.3.2 and 3.3.3).

Categories of possible answers:

a) User has to agree to the terms of service. The information about also accepting the privacy policy is included in those terms

b) The information is only presented to the user by means of very small print or is hardly visible at first sight
c) The information is well readable. There is no attempt to hide it
d) The information is emphasised by using a different font colour etc.
e) Other
f) Comment

Example of b):
Doc. 23

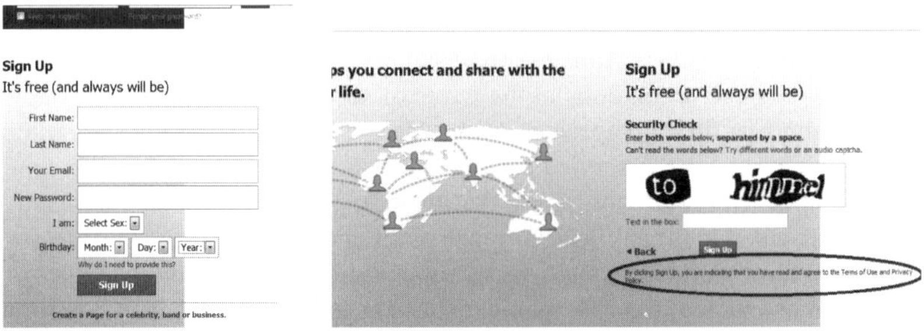

In the initial registration process, the user is not asked to accept any privacy policy (left). However, when he or she is afterwards asked to type in the captcha (right), the user is only informed by small print that he or she is about to consent to the privacy policy. Similar cases are to be categorized under category b). This is due to the fact that the information is only given in the second step where the user would not necessarily expect it and to the fact that the warning is only written in small print

Example of c):

If a different colour were not used in example d), that website could be categorised under category c), as a reasonable font size is used and the warning is not hidden. See below.

Example of d):

Doc. 24

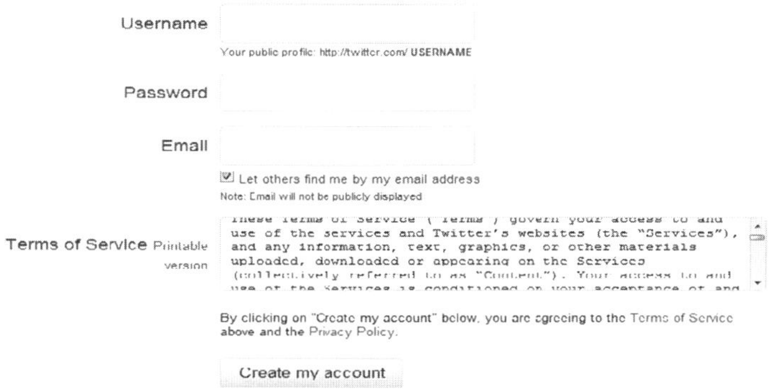

Note: This screenshot is only displayed very small; the actual font size is bigger.

'Terms of service' and 'privacy policy' are displayed in blue, whereas the rest of the text is black, thus catching the viewer's attention.

3.3.4.2 Results of examination

Doc. 25

Member State	User has to agree to the terms of service. The information about also accepting the privacy policy is included in those terms	The information is only presented to the user by means of very small print or is hardly visible at first sight	The information is well readable. There is no attempt to hide it	The information is emphasised by using a different font colour etc.	Other	N/A (e.g. neither privacy policy nor terms of service exist, there is no information pointing out that the user is consenting; problems answering the question)
Austria	5	1	4	0	0	1
Bulgaria	8	0	0	0	0	1
Czech Republic	8	0	8	0	0	2
Denmark	2	3	0	3	0	0
France	4	0	2	2	0	6
Germany	0	1	9	7	0	3
Italy	4	0	1	3	0	3
Malta	0	0	0	0	0	1
Netherlands	7	0	3	3	0	1
Poland	6	0	5	2	0	0
Romania	3	0	0	4	0	4
Slovakia	11	0	10	9	0	0
Spain	5	3	0	4	0	0
United Kingdom	9	2	6	4	0	0
International	5	11	3	2	0	1
	77	21	51	43	0	23

The responses submitted to question four of part three of the study entail some surprising elements. Contrary to expectations only a small number of the providers tried to hide the information that users were consenting to some privacy policy by using very small print. The number of services providing well readable information was rather surprising. This can also be said for the number of services using special means like different colours in order to catch the user's attention. Apart from these aspects, it is remarkable that the overall majority of services force users to agree to their terms of service which either entail the privacy policy or state that by accepting the terms of service, one would also agree to a separate privacy policy. Interestingly, this method was predominant in almost all member states, with the exception of the internationally operating services and on a national level, services in Germany and Denmark. This may be due to several reasons, one of the possible causes being the fact that privacy policies are often not segregated from the terms of service. This is supported by the fact that in Bulgaria and the Czech Republic, for instance, where a segregation of both documents hardly exists (see 3.3.3), the users always have to agree to the terms of service; thus also agreeing to the privacy regulations. The situation is similar in France. In most cases, the privacy policy is not separated from the terms of service and normally accepted by agreeing to those. Some services in France, however, do not give any information whatsoever as to the privacy regulations during the process of registration.

However, these observations are not true for all member states in which the privacy policy was predominantly accepted by consenting to the terms of service. In Austria, for instance, the vast majority of services segregate the privacy policy. Nevertheless, the privacy policy is normally accepted by means of agreeing to the terms of service. The situation is also similar in Italy and the Netherlands. A possible explanation for this is that the services have a privacy policy, but only expect the user to be aware of it, but not to accept it. Obviously, this approach is less consumer friendly than other approaches, as users are not inclined to seek information as to the privacy policy. Not having to agree to it, may very well make the privacy policy appear trivial and not important. In contrast to that, explicit consent to the privacy policy might lead to a higher interest in the document. However, the reason for this observation cannot be determined with certainty. The fact that many services do provide well readable information regarding the fact that users are consenting to the privacy policy is caused by the legal requirement of informing the users. Otherwise, there cannot be any consent. However, this approach is more consumer friendly than informing the user via the terms of service. Some other services even emphasize the fact that users are consenting by other means. This is a further concession to consumer protection.

3.3.5 Accessibility of privacy policy

3.3.5.1 Explanation

Another interesting factor that should be looked at more precisely is the accessibility of the privacy policy. How easy is it for the user to access the written privacy policy? This is an important point with respect to users' ability to get acquainted with the privacy policy of the UGC service. In few cases the privacy policy is directly displayed on the registry page. There is a description field that the user can scroll down. The user has an immediate access to the privacy policy and can read it without any circumstances before agreeing to it. In other cases, the access is guaranteed by a direct hyperlink to the privacy policy. In order to read the privacy policy, the user therefore needs only to click on the word 'privacy policy'. A new window opens with the text of the policy. There are also UGC services that provide a link in the terms of service to the privacy policy if the privacy policy is included in the terms of service. In this case it is more complicated for the user to gain access to the privacy policy. Another, intricate way for the user is a hidden direct link to the privacy policy that demands some research on the website to find it. In doing so, it is very improbable that the user will ever read the privacy policy. Very infrequently the user will make an effort to search for the privacy policy with the result that the user is hardly informed and acquainted with the current privacy policy. In the worst case there is no link at all provided by the UGC provider to the privacy policy.

Categories of possible answers:

a) Privacy policy is directly displayed
b) A direct hyperlink to the privacy policy exists
c) The privacy policy can only be accessed via the terms of service
d) There is a hidden direct link to the privacy policy that demands some research on the website to find it
e) There is no link at all to the privacy policy
f) Other
g) Comment

Example of a):

Doc. 26

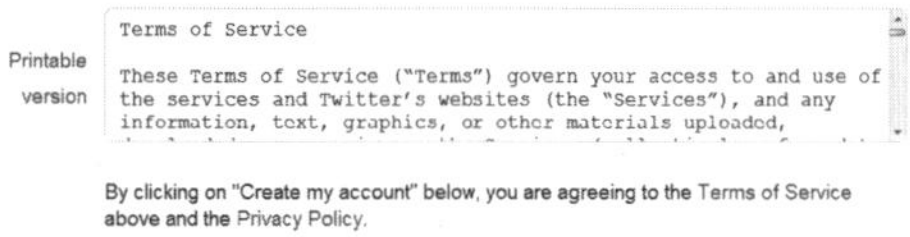

In this example, only the terms of service are directly displayed, but this technical feature could as well be used for the privacy policy.

Explanation of b):

The previous example does also apply here, as there is a direct link to the privacy policy ("privacy policy" at the bottom.)

Explanation of c):

This is to be assumed whenever there is a direct link directing the user to the terms of service. In these terms of service, there must subsequently be another link directing to a separate privacy policy or the privacy policy must be part of the terms of service. If the latter is the case, but there is no direct link to the terms of service during the process of consenting, then the UGC provider was to be categorised under e).

Example of d):

Doc. 27

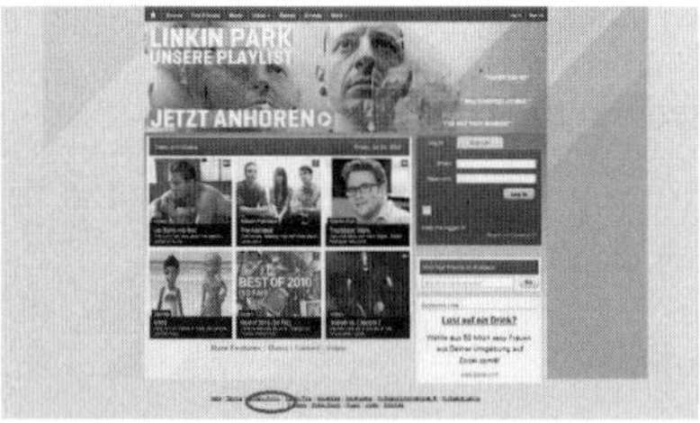

The position of the link to the privacy policy as circled in red is to be categorized under d).

Note: This is only an example of the position of the link on the website.

3.3.5.2 Results of examination

Doc. 28

Member State	Privacy policy is directly displayed	A direct hyperlink to the privacy policy exists	The privacy policy can only be accessed via the terms of service	There is a hidden direct link to the privacy policy that demands some research on the website to find it	There is no link at all to the privacy policy	Other	No privacy policy nor terms of service
Austria	0	5	1	0	0	0	0
Bulgaria	0	1	8	0	0	0	1
Czech Republic	0	1	7	0	0	0	2
Denmark	0	3	3	1	1	0	0
France	0	4	4	0	0	0	0
Germany	0	11	0	1	0	0	2
Italy	0	5	1	0	0	0	2
Malta	0	0	0	0	0	0	1
Netherlands	0	7	2	1	0	0	0
Poland	0	5	2	0	0	0	0
Romania	0	0	3	6	0	0	0
Slovakia	0	3	6	2	0	0	0
Spain	1	8	1	0	0	0	0
United Kingdom	0	9	0	0	1	0	0
International	0	16	0	1	0	0	0
	1	78	38	12	2	0	8

Apart from the fact that some services do not provide a privacy policy at all, it is worth noting that there were providers that have a privacy policy, but do not enable access via the website of the service itself. However, this is an absolute minority, as those make up for only 1% (2 out of 140 services) of the total number of services examined including those services with no privacy policy at all. In contrast to this, the vast majority of services enable the user to access the privacy policy. Some services only feature a hidden direct link that requires some searching to find it (9% of the total services - 12 out of 140). 27% (38 out of 140) allow access only via the terms of service. There are two reasons for this. Some services do not differentiate between the terms of service and the privacy policy at all (see question 3.1.3) while others do differentiate, but choose to allow access only via a link included in the terms of service. The latter services could be driven by an interest in concealing the fact that there is a privacy policy for the same reasons once again; gaining the consent of users who would possible not consent when considering the terms of service. The majority of services provide a simple link to the privacy policy, so they can easily be accessed by the users (56% - 78 out of 140). In this group, the internationally operating services are disproportionately represented once more, with 94% (16 out of 17 international services) of services fulfilling this criterion, whereas only one of those providers had a hidden direct link. This approach can be explained quite easily. A direct hyperlink to the privacy policy is the easiest way for the service provider to fulfil his legal obligation to disclose the regulations to the consumer.

These results here, to a certain extent resemble those of question three: the countries with services which have their privacy policy seperated from the terms of service are also the countries in which most services place direct links to the policy (UK 90%, Germany 79%, Spain 80%, Netherlands 70%). Quite contrary to that group, this was only the case for 10% of the services in Bulgaria, 10% in the Czech Republic, 38% in Denmark and 50% in France. This is clearly related to the question whether the two governing documents are segregated or not. The Spanish service *Tuenti* is the only UGC service under scrutiny that enables the user to directly view the privacy policy while signing up.

3.3.6 Comprehensibility of privacy policy

3.3.6.1 Explanation

It is not only important that users can access the privacy policy but also that they are able to comprehend its content. Therefore, it is important to analyse whether the privacy policy contains native language of the respective target country or whether it is partly or fully in foreign language. The UGC provider cannot assume that all users are capable of speaking another language. Furthermore, it is interesting to ascertain if the privacy policy includes difficult language not suitable for the average user or if it contains simple language which everyone can understand easily. In addition to that it is of high interest whether the privacy policy is written out in detail or whether it is reduced to a reference to the national data protection legislation.

Categories of possible answers:

a) Privacy policy includes foreign language or is completely written in a foreign language
b) Privacy policy contains only native language
c) Privacy policy includes difficult language not suitable to the average user
d) Privacy policy contains simple language for everyone to understand easily
e) Privacy policy itself includes difficult language for the average user but the UGC service provides a link to comprehensive information about data protection
f) Privacy policy is written out in detail
g) Privacy policy is reduced to a reference to the national data protection legislation
h) Other
i) Comment

Explanation: Partners were advised that three answers are mandatory. The text of the privacy policy is either completely composed in the native language or it uses some foreign language or is possibly even completely written in a foreign language. Thus, either a) or b) applies to any UGC service provider. However, in the second step, one has to evaluate the type of language that is used. With regard to c), d) and e), it does not make a difference whether a native or a foreign language is used. The question had to be answered either way. The language is simple when the privacy policy is written in a clear and straightforward manner. On the contrary, the language is especially difficult when the policy is expressed in legal jargon that is difficult for the average user to comprehend. For this part of the question it was recommended that the privacy policy should be read by a layman since most of the partners have studied law and do therefore not represent the average user. Last but not least questions f) and g) belong together.

3.3.6.2 Results of examination

Doc. 29

Name of UGC servic	Privacy policy includes foreign language or is completely written in foreign language	Privacy policy con-tains only native language	Privacy policy includes difficult language not suitable to the average user	Privacy policy contains simple language for everyone to understand easily	Privacy policy itself includes difficult language for the average user but the UGC service provides a link to comprehensiv e information about data protecion	Privacy policy is written out in detail	Privacy policy is reduced to a reference to the national data protection legislation	Other	No privacy policy nor terms of service
Austria	1	5	1	5	0	5	0	0	0
Bulgaria	1	8	0	9	0	5	1	0	1
Czech Republic	0	8	2	6	0	1	3	0	2
Denmark	1	7	6	1	0	1	1	0	0
France	4	4	5	0	3	0	1	0	0
Germany	1	10	3	8	1	5	0	0	2
Italy	3	4	3	2	0	4	2	0	1
Malta	0	0	0	0	0	0	0	0	1
Netherlands	4	6	4	4	2	3	1	0	0
Poland	1	5	0	6	0	4	0	0	0
Romania	3	6	0	9	0	8	1	0	0
Slovakia	5	7	0	9	0	5	0	0	0
Spain	2	8	2	8	0	0	0	0	0
United Kingdom	0	10	0	2	0	3	0	0	0
International	0	0	0	15	1	14	0	0	0
	26	88	26	84	7	58	10	0	7

Dealing with the results of this part of the study, it is important to notice that several services were analyzed in different member states as it was possible that the services use different privacy regulations in the respective countries. This may be caused by a discrepancy in legal requirements in the various countries or by different reactions by consumers in different member states. An example of this is the fact that the terms of service and/or the privacy policy were not translated into the official languages of some countries; but were translated in other languages. It was interesting that there is a significant number of providers that do not write their own privacy policy, but simply refer to the national data protection legislation. This was the case in several member states, but more often in Italy (twice) and in the Czech Republic (three times) than in other member states. This may be due to the fact that the rights of the service providers are clearly defined by those legislations anyway. However, it is also possible that the respective laws grant the services sufficient rights. In contrast, most other services examined had a detailed individual privacy policy that may have included references to data protection legislation, but were not limited to it. However, question 3.3.6. of this part was not limited to that aspect.

7 out of 140 UGC services (5%) neither have a privacy policy nor terms of service. Those seven services were not integrated into the evaluation of question 3.3.6., so that the total number of analyzed services is 133.

Even more significant is the comprehensibility of the policy. The most important aspect of this is probably the language in which the privacy policy is written. Services in the category "international" are not to be adhered, as it was always looked at the English language version in order to be able to compare them more easily. This means that this part of 3.3.6 has a total number of 116 of analyzed services The majority of services supply the users with a privacy policy that contains only the users' native language (75% of the selected services with a policy - 87 out of 116), whereas 22% (26 out of 116 services) of the services use privacy policies that contain at least some foreign language. Providing a privacy policy in the official language of the respective member states is evidently quite important in order to allow the majority of users to understand the policy. In some cases, providers may even be required to do so. Therefore it is not surprising that most services provide such a privacy policy. Looking at the results, it is quite obvious that in some member states substantially more foreign language is used than in others. In the UK and the Czech Republic all services used privacy policies exclusively consisting of native language. In the UK, this is hardly surprising, as English is the language most commonly used in international business, and English is likely to be the standard language of other international services. This seems more surprising regarding the Czech Republic, as Czech is only spoken in that country. However, since none of the selected services in the Czech Republic are international, it would hardly make sense to have a privacy policy in any other language. The situation in Bulgaria (89%) is the same as in the Czech Republic, except that with Wikipedia one international service was also selected. This service however, is the only service using foreign language. The situation in Denmark, where all services except *Facebook* are Danish, mirrors the one in Bulgaria. Here, *Facebook* is the only selected internationally operating service and it is the only one using foreign language. The situation in the Netherlands (60%) is similar as well. The reason for the fact that the percentage of native language is so small is that in the Netherlands, there were significantly more international UGC services than in the Czech Republic, for example. Some of them like *Twitter*, did not offer a Dutch language version. However *Wikipedia*, also an international service, did. In Slovakia, another relatively small member state, none of the international services offered a full Slovak language version of the privacy policy and one exclusively Slovakian provider surprisingly also used foreign language. In contrast to this, the situation in other member states differs significantly. In Spain for example, 80% of the selected services used native language only. The two services that did not were international. Nevertheless, there were other internationally operating services that did offer a Spanish language version. This includes *Facebook, Myspace* and *Youtube*, for instance. It is worth noting that *Facebook* does not offer a Slovak language version. The situation is quite similar in Germany, where 91% of the services use native language only with *Twitter* being the only service using English in parts of the privacy policy. A possible explanation for this phenomenon is the plain fact that there are significantly more speakers of German and Spanish than there are of Slovakian or Danish. Thus, translating the privacy policy does not always make sense when only few new consumers can be reached by doing so. This is very likely the result of an economic decision.

The last aspect of question six was whether the privacy policy is written in a rather technical or legal language or simple language that is easily understood by an average user. In contrast to the previous aspect of question six, this part contains the category of internationally operating services. Surprisingly, roughly 63% (84 out of 133) of all services used simple language in their privacy policies, thus making it quite easy for consumers to understand the provisions. However, it is important to keep in mind that there are also other factors that contribute to the comprehensibility of a privacy policy such as its length, which may incline users to actually read it or not. Around 20% (58 out of 133) of the services used very difficult language and did not help users with the understanding. This was the case quite often in Denmark, France, Italy and the Netherlands. However, there were also some services that offered a complicated legal framework, but did provide simplified explanations (5% - 7 out of 133). Interestingly, this approach was mainly found only in France and in the Netherlands. Moreover, some services have a policy in rather simple language, but also offer further simplifications. Generally, one would assume that the number of services using technical language would have been greater. However, this is not the case. This may be due to the fact that most privacy policies simply state what the service providers can and cannot do with the user data. Therefore technical legal language is normally not necessary. However, providers may use technical language to obscure the purposes for which they collect and use data and the right that they have to use these data.

3.3.7 Length of privacy policy

3.3.7.1 Explanation

Additionally, the length of the privacy policy is also of great interest. A privacy policy that consists of many pages is very unlikely to be read by many users. The average user might not be willing to spend plenty of time reading it carefully and in detail. Therefore it is important that the provider summarises and centralises the content of the privacy policy to a length that is most likely to be read by the user. In contrast, it will be interesting to see whether the UGC provider uses extensive privacy policy or not. In order to draw conclusions as to this criterion, we asked our partners to count the number of words that the privacy policy consists of. By counting the words we can take into consideration that each language might have a different average amount of words. This could have been done, for instance, by copying and pasting the policy in Word and using the feature 'word count'.

3.3.7.2 Results of examination

Doc. 30

Member State	Average number of words
Austria	3034
Bulgaria	728
Czech Republic	233
Denmark	1240
France	1542
Germany	1513
Italy	1090
Malta	0
Netherlands	1216
Poland	808
Romania	1237
Slovakia	1212
Spain	3328
United Kingdom	2361
International	2862
	0

Regarding this aspect of practices used by providers, the variety of approaches catches the viewer's attention immediately. Disregarding those UGCs that do not have any privacy policy at all, the length of the privacy policies varied significantly. While one service has a privacy policy that is limited to 45 words, the most extensive policy consisted of no less than 7,500 words. One has to note that some differences among the various member states may be explained by the differences in languages. However, this is not always the case.

Internationally operating services used privacy policies with an average length of about 2,900 words (in the UK 2,400 words, in Germany 1,800 words). The services selected in Romania use privacy policies 1200 words long on average. Spain is not a good example when looking for possible regional differences as all services are internationally operating. Noteworthy may be however that "*Tuenti*", the Spain-based internationally operating service, has with its 7536 words the most extensive privacy policy of all services under scrutiny.

At first sight, it does not seem to be unusual that Slovakia's privacy policies entail the same number on average. However, when taking a closer look at Slovakia, it becomes obvious that only those services that are internationally active have extensive policies. When only considering the *.sk* services, the average number of words is approximately 150. With services like *Facebook* using about 40 times as many words, it can be ruled out that this is caused by the difference in languages. In Italy, the situation is somewhat like the one in Slovakia, with the average number of words being about 1,200. However, when the international service *lastfm* is excluded from the Italian examined UGC services, the average number of words is not even 800, which is significantly less when compared to the member states named above. In Poland, the average number of words is about 800. This is also quite short, but there are no such anomalies as in Slovakia or Italy, since all services are *.pl* websites.

Generally, it can be observed that the international services do have more extensive privacy policies than those services only operating nationally. This becomes obvious when looking at the category of international services, but also when looking at some member states in which international services were also under scrutiny such as Slovakia or Italy. Also in Spain, the average number of words is significantly greater than in most other member states. Regarding Spain, one needs to keep in mind that all Spanish services were internationally operating.

Furthermore, a significant discovery is that privacy policies were often more extensive when they were segregated from the terms of service. For instance, in the Czech Republic where almost all services did not segregate the privacy policy and terms of service, the average number of words - not considering services without any policy and services with a separate privacy policy - was only 235. While in Bulgaria that number was 650, it was slightly over 800 when considering *bg.Wikipedia* with a segregated policy.

However, this observation is not true with respect to all member states. In Denmark for instance, *alatest.dk* had a very short privacy policy of only 300 words that was integrated in the terms of service. Nevertheless, the service using the shortest privacy policy with only 150 words had a segregated privacy policy. In contrast to that, the observation does have more credibility in Italy, where the two shortest privacy regulations with less than 50 words were integrated in the terms of service. Poland also confirms the observation. All but two Polish services used segregated privacy policies. Compared with other member states the overall average for Poland seems rather small, but the two really short privacy policies (99 and 276 words) that have a great impact on the average are services that do not segregate the privacy policy from the terms of service. Without those two services, Poland would average more than 1,100 words. Finally, in Romania, this assumption seems to be accurate as well, as the average was 1,200 words, but the three shortest policies were integrated, only averaging 340 words.

The fact that very short privacy policies are not being used by international providers, but by various national service providers can be explained by a lack of legal know-how by some of the national providers. National providers tend to be rather small in comparison with international providers. Therefore, it is not uncommon that they have smaller resources and cannot spend as much money for legal services as big international service providers. A result of this is a lack of a well-designed privacy policy. The reason is therefore rather economic. Nevertheless, this is not the only reason. It is also likely that the effectiveness of consumer protection varies once more.

3.3.8 Boldface, colours and other means to facilitate the reading and understanding of the privacy policy

3.3.8.1 Explanation

This criterion, similar to some of the previously established criteria refers to the text of the privacy policy itself. It also relates to the comprehensibility of the privacy policy. The users need to be able to understand what they are consenting to, in order for their consent to be reasonable. This criterion was meant to include various approaches that may make it substantially easier for users to understand the privacy policy. This may be done by means of boldface, different colours to emphasise important parts etc.

Categories of possible answers:

a) Use of boldface (except in headlines)
b) Emphasis of relevant parts by using another colour or by other means (except hyperlinks)
c) Division into several sections (in contrast to one long running text)
d) Use of headlines
e) Does the text include links to further relevant information/explanations/settings?

f) Is there an e-mail-address for the purpose of contacting the service provider with any questions and/or queries on the privacy policy?
g) Other
h) Comment

3.3.8.2 Results of examination

Doc. 31

Name of UGC service	Use of boldface (except in headlines)	Emphasis of relevant parts by using another colour or by other means (except hyperlinks)	Division into several sections (in contrast to one long running text)	Use of headlines	Does the text include links to further relevant information/explanations/settings?	Is there an e-mail-address for the purpose of contacting the service provider with any questions and/or querie…	No features at all	No privacy policy nor terms of service
Austria	2	3	6	6	5	5	0	0
Bulgaria	1	0	3	6	1	5	0	1
Czech Republic	0	0	7	1	0	2	0	2
Denmark	2	1	5	5	4	1	1	0
France	0	0	4	8	3	2	0	0
Germany	5	4	12	9	9	8	0	2
Italy	1	0	4	4	2	2	4	0
Malta	0	0	0	0	0	0	0	1
Netherlands	3	2	9	7	5	7	0	0
Poland	3	1	5	6	3	1	0	0
Romania	0	3	9	9	2	5	0	0
Slovakia	5	4	8	6	3	2	0	0
Spain	2	2	10	9	10	5	0	0
United Kingdom	1	3	10	10	1	10	0	0
International	1	3	17	17	10	12	0	0
	26	26	109	103	58	67	5	6

Looking at the results regarding question eight of part three it is interesting to see that apart from six UGC services (4%) that do not offer neither a privacy policy nor terms of service, five out of 140 analysed UGC services (which means 4%) have either a privacy policy or terms of service that include a privacy policy but do not use any specific feature in order to facilitate the reading and understanding of the privacy policy.

On the other hand 92% of all the UGC services use various approaches to make it substantially easier for users to understand the privacy policy. Most frequently used is the approach through division into several sections (109 out of 129 UGC services that use specific features) and the use of headlines (103 out of 129 UGC services). Additionally, 67 UGC services provide an e-mail-address for the purpose of contacting the service provider with any questions and/or queries on the privacy policy. Sometimes it is even the case that the UGC service includes the full adress of the provider (see *hi5* Slovakia).

Features that are not as commonly used as the above mentioned are the use of boldface outside the headline (20% - 26 out of 129) and the use of different colour, font or other accentuations (20% - 26 out of 129).
The methods used by the providers are almost all quite consumer-friendly. Almost all service providers do something to facilitate the reading of the privacy

policy. However, the means by which they do so clearly show that costs play an important role. While it does not require much work to divide the privacy policy into several sections or to use headlines, it is more work-intensive to provide an e-mail address for further question. This is due to the fact that by doing so it is also required to have a qualified employee or contractor available to respond to those e-mails. This creates costs. It is also quite uncommon that further information is given. This can also be explained by the fact that it is relatively cost-intensive. Therefore it is no surprise that *Facebook* as the most influential UGC service provider is able to do so. This is also true as to the usage of boldface and different colours outside of headlines. Using these means requires an evaluation by a qualified person, considering which parts of the privacy policy are legally important. Furthermore, the interests of the service provider could not be forgotten. Thus, the service provider may still want not to emphasize some relevant information for the provider's sake.

3.3.9 Process of amending the privacy policy

3.3.9.1 Explanation

All the previously discussed criteria dealt with the process of how user consent is obtained in the first place. However, once the user has granted his or her consent, the UGC provider may be willing to change the service's privacy policy. If user consent is not to be completely meaningless, the individual users would have to agree to the changed terms as well. As in the process of newly obtaining user consent, the means that are being used in order to gain renewed user consent vary severely amongst different providers. The first subject of interest was therefore how users are informed of an intended change of the privacy policy. Some providers do not inform users at all, except for changing the accessible privacy policy, thus hardly giving users the chance of being aware of the changes made. Other services may actually inform the user via e-mail. These differences in dealing with privacy policy changes are of great importance, because by later changes, providers have as much influence on the rules as through the initial process. Information regarding this can most likely be found in the privacy policy itself or in the terms of service. If located in the terms of service, the information will probably be incorporated in the section dealing with changes to the terms. If there was no information about the process of amending the privacy policy in the privacy policy itself or in the terms of service it was recommended to the partners to contact the UGC service provider and ask how they deal with the aspect.

Categories of possible answers:

a) The user usually receives no special notification regarding the changes
b) Information about the changes is displayed on the website
c) The user is informed via e-mail
d) Other

e) Comment

Explanation of a):

This category was to include cases in which the accessible privacy policy was only updated, but users were not notified of those changes.

Explanation of b):

There might be a link on the website or similar hints at the changes. This category was also to include websites that require the user to take further steps in order to receive information by the provider. An example of this could be *Facebook* that requires users to become a "fan" of a certain page in order to receive information on policy updates.

3.3.9.2 Results of examination

Doc. 32

Member State	The user usually receives no special notification regarding the changes	Information about the changes is displayed on the website	The user is informed via e-mail	No relevant information available	No privacy policy nor terms of service
Austria	0	0	6	0	0
Bulgaria	1	3	2	3	1
Czech Republic	7	1	0	0	2
Denmark	6	1	1	0	0
France	0	8	0	1	0
Germany	3	2	3	5	2
Italy	2	0	0	7	0
Malta	0	0	0	0	1
Netherlands	5	5	2	0	1
Poland	2	4	3	0	0
Romania	7	1	1	1	0
Slovakia	11	1	1	0	0
Spain	6	4	2	0	0
United Kingdom	0	10	1	0	0
International	8	8	5	0	0
	58	48	27	17	6

The examination of this question has shown that the management of the process of amending the privacy policy is handled very differently from UGC service to UGC service. Firstly, it has to be taken into account that six UGC services do not provide a privacy policy or terms of service at all. Secondly, and very surprisingly, 17 out of 140 UGC services (12%) do not provide any relevant information available on how they deal with amendments to their privacy policy. Especially in Italy (78%), Germany (36%) and Bulgaria (30%) there was often no information to be found on the UGC services to that question. In Germany the information that could be found did not deal with the privacy policy, but only with changes to the terms of service. Regarding the first three possibilities the answers are very distributed. 41% (58 out of 140) of the UGC services do not give the user any form of special notification regarding changes to their privacy policy. In particular, the majority of the analysed UGC services in Slovakia (85%), Romania (70%), Czech Republic (70%) and Denmark (75%) do not provide any information about changes of the privacy policy. This reveals that more than one third of the analysed UGC services do not inform the user at all about changes of the privacy policy. This matter can easily be explained by the fact that service provider do not have any interest in an informed consumer. If the provider does inform the consumer, he or she may become dissatisfied with the changes and decide to leave the service. However, this is not in the interest of services, because fewer users can lead to less income from advertising etc.

If information about amendments regarding the privacy policy is provided the UGC service provider may use two different methods: He is either displaying the information about the changes on the website or he is informing the user by sending him or her an email. The results of the research show that 48 out of 140 UGC services (34%) prefer to display the information about the changes on the website while only 27 out of 140 UGC services (19%) inform the user directly via e-mail. With displaying the information on the website the user runs the risk of not noticing the changes to the privacy policy. This is done by the providers for the same reasons as stated above. Service providers do not have any interest in users realizing that the privacy policy has changed.

3.3.10 How is consent obtained when amending the privacy policy?

3.3.10.1 Explanation

In 3.3.9, the subject of interest was the way users were informed of intended changes to the privacy policy. However, the process of amending the privacy policy is not only limited to informing users about those changes, they also have to consent to those changes. Once again many different approaches are used in order to obtain consent. This is partly done by stating that the continued use of the services constitutes consent. This approach, for instance, may be critical to users' consent, because it is not necessary to actively do anything. Basically, users' consent is feigned. This can be additionally problematic if users have not been personally informed. In contrast, an explicit consent may be required for the user in order to continue using the service. This means of obtaining consent is much more an actual conscious consent than the former. One can conclude that many different options are available and it appears necessary to conduct an examination of those, as they are substantially related to the fact of obtaining consent. The content of the privacy policy and of the terms of service was of high interest. This is due to the fact that the process of amending the privacy policy is likely to be regulated in either one of them. Partners could find the information required to answer the question in either the terms of service or in the privacy policy. Where this was not the case partners were asked to contact the stakeholder and ask for the information needed.

Categories of possible answers:

a) Opt-out–process is used. The user accepts changes by not doing anything
b) The user has to explicitly consent to the changes (opt-in)
c) Other
d) Comment

Explanation of b):

For instance, this could be done by means of a pop-up-window on the website, by an e-mail that would require the user to click on a link in order to consent to the changes etc.

3.3.10.2 Results of examination

Doc. 33

Member State	Opt-out –process is used. The user accepts changes by not doing anything	The user has to explicitly consent to the changes (opt-in)	Other	No information given	No privacy policy nor terms of service
Austria	6	0	0	0	0
Bulgaria	6	0	0	3	1
Czech Republic	7	1	0	0	2
Denmark	5	3	0	0	0
France	7	0	0	1	0
Germany	5	0	1	5	2
Italy	3	0	0	6	0
Malta	0	0	0	0	1
Netherlands	8	1	0	1	0
Poland	3	3	0	0	
Romania	8	0	0	0	0
Slovakia	12	0	0	0	0
Spain	10	0	0	0	0
United Kingdom	10	0	0	0	0
International	12	0	1	4	0
	102	8	2	20	6

As one can see on the chart, the vast majority of the analysed UGC services use the opt-out method in order to receive users consent. This was the case with 102 out of 140 analysed UGC services (73%). Service providers tend to use this means for several reasons. One important advantage of this approach is the fact that it is the easiest way to receive consent. Furthermore, many users will not do anything for a lack of interest. Thus, this approach really helps the service providers. Only a very small minority (6 % - 8 out of 140) uses the opt-in method where the user actively has to do something in order to consent to the changes. The opt-in-process is mainly used in Poland (3) and Denmark (3). Additionally, the opt-in-process can be found once in the Netherlands and in Czech Republic. Extraordinary is the fact that 14% (20 out of 140) of all UGC services do not give any information about how consent is obtained when amending the privacy policy. As in question 3.3.9 especially the analysed UGC services in Italy (67%), Germany (36%) and Bulgaria (30%) refrain from informing the user properly: they do not give any information on this question. Furthermore, six UGC services provide neither a privacy policy nor terms of service (4% - 6 out of 140 UGC services). In addition to that, *Facebook* uses quite an interesting method. In general, no consent is obtained from the user concerning changes to the privacy policy. However, if more than 7000 users comment on the proposed change *Facebook* will give users the opportunity to participate in a vote in which user will be provided with alternatives. The change voted for is binding on *Facebook* if more than 30% of all active registered users as of the date of the notice vote. Considering the number of users of *Facebook,* it becomes quite clear that this required 30 % will never be achieved. Thus this clause is only included in the regulations in order to appease its critics. In fact, *Facebook* still has the power to impose any policies on its user whether they like it or not.

Regarding the UGC services that use the opt-out-process the time in which the user can disagree to the changes vary between two to six weeks. After that period of time it is assumed that the user agrees to the changes by continuing to use the service. Sometimes, such a period of time does not exist at all. In fact the user agrees by continuing to use the service after the changes. Thus, those changes are virtually accepted instantly.

4. Conclusion and Future Prospects

The evaluation of the questionnaires gave an insight into the common purposes for which UGC service providers collect, use and disclose users´ personal data (part 1), the extent to which users may refuse or withdraw such consent (part 2) the current policies and practices among UGC service providers for obtaining users' consent (part 3).

The first part of the survey enumerated the main purposes for which UGC service providers collect and process user data. Not surprisingly, almost all of the 140 UGC websites asked for certain personal data with a view to contact users or to enable features on the website to function. More interestingly half of the websites in question stated openly that one of their main purposes was to profile the user in order to make profit. The dark figure might be higher, but even the percentage found by this research was respectable. So, one might think that there is "nothing wrong" about collecting data in order to make profit as long as he or she is told about this purpose. Being an informed user does not necessarily mean being a user who criticizes any usage of the data. But the study revealed that an unequally high number of websites tried to obscure this very purpose in comparison to other purposes (no one tried to obscure the purpose of fulfilling legal obligations for example). This shows the huge intrinsic financial potential of profiling users. Though the majority of UGC service providers divided the privacy policy in several sections to facilitate the reading, this division is of no advantage if the average user does not understand the content of the text. It is highly doubtable if the reader of such a privacy policy can be really considered "informed". Regarding the usage of different data it is striking that almost 30 percent of the collected personal information is used to profile the user in the view to make profit. Personal information includes religious beliefs, political opinion, family, relationship status, hobbies, etc, ergo information that is normally provided voluntarily. Interestingly, all the other data (date of birth, employment information etc) are used for profiling users as well. Therefore, it is possible to say that profiling users with a view to make profit is one of the most important purposes with respect to the collection of data. The business models regarding the collecting, using and disclosing of personal data should be subject of further surveys in other research projects. Eminently, one will have to estimate what role data protection plays in those business models. The service providers need the money they make with selling users' personal data. Thus, how can decision makers ensure data protection without impairing economic growth? Finding an answer to this question will be the main task for the legislature in the future. Do we want the maximum protection with the risk of a financial collapse of service providers? Although there might be a lot of open questions and work to do for the legislator, the current practice of service providers of obscuring their purpose cannot be tolerated.

Another problem of data policies was revealed in Part 2 and 3 of this research. When being asked to agree to the privacy policy of the website in question, one might wonder about the consequences of disagreeing. Does the user still have the possibility to use the service? When defining "consent" as mentioned in the beginning, one could think that the most important part of the definition is the "voluntary" agreement to the proposal of another. The survey showed a clear result: Not granting consent, withdrawing consent or not agreeing to changes to the privacy policy have mostly one consequence: The denial of using the service. This "sink or swim" approach certainly works best to get the most data possible. The pressure to agree to the policy in order to stay in contact with friends or family and to participate in the respective UGC service is a very persuasive means. Speaking of "consent" in this context could be the wrong word. Consent in its legal meaning emphasizes the voluntariness of the decision. On the other hand it is the service provider who sells his service. The user "pays" for it by agreeing to the usage of his data. The possibility of using facebook or StudiVZ is not a public service. So should the service provider be allowed to ask for any data he wants? Answering with a clear "no" is a solution that holds a high financial risk for the provider. In fact, one has to approach the problem from a different view – the user. If the user is properly informed about the usage of his data and the fact that he "pays" for the service with the release of his personal information the legislator should not impair. Means to ensure that the user reads the privacy policy are using a blank checkbox in order to grant consent and then click register ("opt-in" method) and separating the policy from the terms of service. Another effective instrument is the length of the privacy policy itself. The shorter the likelier it is that the user reads it. The Europe-wide comparison showed that Germany holds a pioneering role in this context. Most German service providers use a well-readable, short and non-hidden privacy policy.

Nevertheless, balancing the interests of users and service providers will be the main task for legislators, but also for service providers themselves in the future.